MYSTER
AT GREENFINGERS

A Comedy of Detection

by
J. B. PRIESTLEY

SAMUEL FRENCH

LONDON
NEW YORK SYDNEY TORONTO HOLLYWOOD

Please see page iv for further copyright information

MYSTERY AT GREENFINGERS

Produced at the Fortune Theatre, London, W.C.2, on January 18th, 1938, by the Bournemouth Little Theatre Club, winners of the " NEWS CHRONICLE " Amateur Dramatic Contest, 1937–38, with the following cast of characters :

(In the order of their appearance)

ARNOLD JORDAN	.	.	.	.	. *James Emerson.*
EDNA SANDARS	.	.	.	.	. *Kathleen Wiseman.*
KEITH HENLEY	.	.	.	.	. *Herbert Wiseman.*
HELEN TENNANT	.	.	.	.	. *Heather Taylor.*
SALLY PHILIPS	.	.	.	.	. *Kitty Heane.*
CLARA PACKER	.	.	.	.	. *Joan Homer.*
ROSE HEATON	.	.	.	.	. *Myrtle Moss.*
FRED POOLE	.	.	.	.	. *Geoffrey Harding.*
ROBERT CROWTHER	.	.	.	.	. *Geoffrey Baverstock.*
MISS TRACEY	.	.	.	.	. *Dorothy Rowe.*

The Play produced by PHILIP TAYLOR.

The scene throughout is one of the staff rooms of the large Greenfingers Palace Hotel, in the Peak District.

ACT   I.—An evening in March, about a fortnight before Easter.
ACT II.—Next morning.
ACT III.—That afternoon.

NOTES ON CHARACTERS

MISS TRACEY (an elderly spinster, a lady of independent means from Storton-under-the-Hill, Gloucestershire. She is very lively, intelligent, downright, with a sharp staccato manner of speech. She is dressed throughout in sensible travelling tweeds).

HELEN TENNANT (about twenty-five, pretty, and with pleasant manners. She is the games and social hostess of the hotel. Dressed throughout in winter-day clothes, rather " sporting " in type. Preferably fair).

EDNA SANDARS (a bookkeeper and secretary, about twenty-seven or twenty-eight, and preferably dark and rather sleek. Sometimes wears very smart spectacles. Rather hard and sharp. Quite smartly dressed, in darkish clothes).

MRS. (ROSE) HEATON (staff manageress of the hotel. About thirty-five, rather handsome, quiet, efficient, reserved, rather bitter in manner. She is already wearing her uniform, which is a smart black outfit).

SALLY PHILIPS (one of the hotel company's more experienced maids. About twenty-seven. Rather " tough " in manner, sharp-witted, cynical. Quite nice-looking. Wears the hotel maids' uniform, which should be quite attractive).

CLARA PACKER (another maid, younger and far less sophisticated than Sally. Wears same uniform. A simple, good-hearted creature).

KEITH HENLEY (assistant manager of the hotel. About twenty-eight. Good-looking nice young man, with good social background. Keen on his job. Wears ordinary good clothes, not the black coat, etc., he will wear when hotel is open).

ARNOLD JORDAN (one of the hotel chefs. About forty-five. Preferably large and rather fat. Is half-French, and talks with faint French accent, using the French " r." Good-natured, amusing, but temperamental. Wears ordinary good clothes, but can be seen once wearing chef's cap and apron).

7

FRED POOLE (the cocktail barman of the hotel. About thirty. Very sleek and smart, and affects slight American style of speech above his native Cockney. Nattily dressed, but wears a white uniform jacket of cocktail barman instead of ordinary lounge coat).

ROBERT CROWTHER (the hotel company's detective. An ex-Scotland Yard officer. About fifty. Preferably tall, heavy, rather military figure. Wears ordinary clothes. Still the self-important policeman, with loud voice and heavy-handed manner).

NOTE

This play was carefully devised and specially written as a test piece for amateur dramatic societies competing in the " NEWS CHRONICLE " Drama Contest, 1937–38. Its single set, properties, costumes, are the simplest possible. It requires no elaborate effects. All it demands are sensible lively production and good acting. The author has put it into the form of a detective play —though it contains no murders and no police—for two reasons: firstly, because the general public likes this type of play; secondly because it is easier to produce and act a play with a certain obvious plot structure than it is to do a play of pure character. Nevertheless, this is really a comedy of character, masquerading as—and to some extent burlesquing—a mystery play. The producer should remember this, and should make his characters more authentic than the plot.

This Acting Edition has been prepared from the prompt copy used by the Bournemouth Little Theatre Club, winners of the Contest, January, 1938.

MYSTERY AT GREENFINGERS

ACT I

The SCENE *throughout is one of the staff rooms of the large Greenfingers Palace Hotel, in the Peak District. It is a perfectly simple rectangular room, new and rather bare, in the modern manner, and impersonal, as such rooms always are.*

It has no outer window at all, and is obviously artificially ventilated. But on the L. *wall, running all along, to the height of about seven feet, there are windows of thick opaque glass, which admit some light from the corridor outside. Up* L. *is the door leading to the main part of the hotel. On the* R. *wall is the door leading to the kitchen and some of the other staff quarters. The furniture consists of a fair-sized table and plenty of light chairs. (No big easy chairs.) On the* L. *wall above the small table there is a notice-board with various notices and STAFF REGULATIONS, also a letter rack with one or two odd letters in. On the* R. *wall is another framed notice headed IN CASE OF FIRE. The woodwork throughout the set should be painted as light as possible. Some introduction of glass, chromium plate, etc., to suggest that the hotel is very modern, would be effective. The lighting should be plain and rather bright. The floor should be covered with brown linoleum or something of that kind. The general effect of the room should be new, clean, bright, but rather bare and comfortless.*

At rise of CURTAIN *we hear an operatic tenor singing at full blast.* JORDAN *is standing in front of back wall* R., *apparently singing very dramatically—though actually he is only imitating an operatic singer, opening his mouth and making gestures but not singing himself.*

11

The table is set with remains of supper for five. EDNA
SANDARS *is sitting above the table, nearer to* KEITH,
who is at the L. *end.* HELEN *is sitting below the table,
slightly* R.C. SALLY *and* CLARA *are clearing the table,
but have halted to watch* JORDAN'S *performance, and
stand grinning,* SALLY *up by the sideboard,* CLARA *with
a full tray stopped at door* R. *They are all amused.*
EDNA *and* KEITH *are smoking.* JORDAN *continues his
performance until* MRS. HEATON *enters* L. *She stands
and looks contemptuously at him, and when he sees her
look, he suddenly stops, looking sheepish, moves away,
and then we see that he has been standing in front of
a radio set against the back wall* R.C. *He turns round,
and to hide his embarrassment, begins fiddling with the
set, first turning off the station that had produced the
tenor.* SALLY *continues to clear the table ;* CLARA *goes
out* R.

MRS. HEATON (*scornfully*). I'm sorry to interrupt
your performance, Mr. Jordan.

(*His back is eloquent, but he does not reply.*)

EDNA (*with irony*). You were quite right, Mrs.
Heaton. We nearly had some fun then. Another
minute and we'd have been laughing. One has to be
careful, hasn't one ?

MRS. HEATON (*calmly*). I'm here to get on with my
work, Miss Sandars. And I came in to ask you to come
up to the linen-room. I want you to check my figures.

(ARNOLD *sits in the upstage chair* R. *and reads the* " *Radio
Times.*")

EDNA (*grumbling*). What, at this time ? Have a
heart ! I've been checking everybody's figures all day,
and nearly died of cold.

KEITH (*protesting*). You're not going on to-night,
are you, Mrs. Heaton ?

(CLARA *enters* R. *with an empty tray.*)

MRS. HEATON. I'm sorry, Mr. Henley, but I really must.

(ARNOLD, *still seated, starts to tune the wireless set.*)

We're hopelessly short, and Mr. Chadwick specially asked me to let him know what I needed as soon as ever possible.

EDNA (*rising slowly and moving down* L. *to the small table*). Oh—all right. But if I die of pneumonia here, send my body back to town, will you?

HELEN (*sweetly*). I've some notes for you too, Miss Sandars. But I can give them to you down here afterwards.

EDNA (*with cheerful rudeness, turning up to the door* L.). Can't you tell them yourself you're two ping-pong balls and a bridge table short?

KEITH (*annoyed with her*). That'll do.

EDNA. Yes, won't it?

(*She is about to move off when the wireless set begins announcing the news.* JORDAN *steps to one side of it, and, watching it, begins lighting a cigarette.* EDNA *stops to listen.*)

VOICE FROM SET (*very unctuous*). . . . copyright reserved. The weather. (*The* ANNOUNCER *has a nasty attack of coughing.*)

SALLY (*stopping to listen*). Well, what about it?

VOICE FROM SET. I beg your pardon. Snow is still falling in the North and the Midlands, and already there are very high drifts in the Lake District, North Yorkshire and the Peak District. The Post Office reports that some telegraph and telephone lines in one or two districts in Westmorland, Cumberland and Derbyshire are now out of action. The Automobile Association have asked all members who propose travelling through the higher Midlands and the North to ask advice before venturing on any but main roads. This is the heaviest fall of snow recorded in March for the last fifty-one years. . . Roumania. The government crisis in Roumania——

EDNA (*loudly*). No, not Roumania.

KEITH. Turn it off, Arnold.

(JORDAN *turns off the set and sits on the downstage chair* R.)

JORDAN (*with droll despair*). More and more snow!

And in less than a fortnight they think they open this hotel.

EDNA. By that time, they'll be just about trying to dig us out. Or sending St. Bernard dogs to look for us.

KEITH. I say, I suppose our telephone line's all right? Anybody tried it lately?

JORDAN. That engineer—what's his name?—Burton —used it this morning, just before he left. I was with him.

EDNA. That's the last voice they'll probably ever hear from the Greenfingers Palace Hotel.

MRS. HEATON. I'll see if it's all right.

(She goes out L. CLARA and SALLY are both at the sideboard.)

SALLY. I looked out of a window a bit since, Mr. Henley, and I couldn't see anything for snow.

CLARA *(supporting her)*. Oo—yes. I never saw so much.

HELEN *(laughing, mostly to KEITH)*. We'll have to have winter sports. *(She moves to small table R.)*

KEITH. Good idea! Well, we're easily the highest big hotel in England We're nearly fifteen hundred feet up.

EDNA. Is that all? It feels like fifteen thousand. *(She comes to L.C. above the table.)*

SALLY *(sarcastically, as she takes a dish away)*. Yes, I'll bet it's cold up here in winter.

CLARA *(innocently, to her)*. Well, I call it winter now, don't you?

SALLY. We can't keep anything hidden from you, can we?

(She goes out R., followed by CLARA. MRS. HEATON enters L., looking rather depressed.)

KEITH. What about it, Mrs. Heaton?

MRS. HEATON. No, the 'phone's quite dead.

KEITH. Are you sure?

MRS. HEATON. Yes. Something must have happened to the line. Are you ready, Miss Sandars?

EDNA (*pushing her chair in*). What, are you still
going on with your stocktaking ?

MRS. HEATON. Why not ?

EDNA (*dramatically*). Snowed up ! Cut off from the
world ! And we're still counting sheets and pillow-
cases !

(*She and* MRS. HEATON *go out* L. JORDAN, *who is slumped,
gloomily smoking, groans.* HELEN, *who is now standing
above the small table* R., *picks up the paper.*)

JORDAN. Keith, my friend, I told you this place was
all wrong.

KEITH. We did good business here last season.

JORDAN (*with mock despair*). This season they won't
find us until the end of June. And what old Marini
will say when he finds himself up here, after Bournemouth, and with that kitchen to run—and eight miles
from a railway station, and a bad service—everything
to be ordered so long in advance—he'll go back to Italy
and take his chance with Mussolini. He's the best chef
the company has, too. And I am the next best. They
might as well have sent us to Greenland.

KEITH. I like that ! And Chadwick told me you
specially asked to come here this season.

JORDAN (*gloomily, moving to* R. *of the table*). That's
because I'm a fool, Keith. Every year I do one big
damn silly thing. This year I got it in early. I asked
to come here.

(*Enter* FRED POOLE *from* L. *He is carrying a bottle
wrapped in tissue-paper.*)

FRED (*handing over the bottle*). Here you are, Mr.
Jordan. I think this is what you wanted. Will you
sign for it ?

(JORDAN *signs a chit at the sideboard.*)

KEITH (*to* HELEN). This is Fred, best cocktail-bar
man in the company.

HELEN (*to* FRED). Oh, yes—we've met before,

haven't we ? You were down at Cannes, when I went
to help Mrs. Morrison there, last season.

FRED (*crossing to* HELEN). That's right. Miss
Tennant, isn't it ? How d'you like it up here ? Change
from Cannes, all right, eh ?

HELEN. Yes. But it's my first chance as hostess
on my own, so I can't grumble. But why did you leave
Cannes ?

FRED (*jauntily*). Oh—like to move round a bit,
y'know, Miss Tennant. Don't make much money, but
we do see life, eh ?

JORDAN (*gloomily, coming to* L. *of* FRED). When do
you think you will see life here, Fred ?

FRED (*grinning*). You have a good pull at that bottle,
Mr. Jordan, and you'll see anything you want to see.

KEITH. Here, what's he got there ?

JORDAN (*deliberately*). Old rum—very old rum.

KEITH (*with mock alarm*). Hoy, steady !

JORDAN. When things are so bad, they cannot be
any worse, I drink old rum. I think I will go round
that kitchen once again, and then drink myself unconscious. (*He moves towards the door* R.)

KEITH. If it's half as bad as you say it is, you'd better
let me have a full report in the morning.

JORDAN. I will write it in rum and blood and tears.

(*He goes out* R.)

FRED. Only about half my stuff's here, Mr. Henley.
I'd better get through to head office first thing in the
morning.

KEITH. If you can.

FRED. Why not ?

KEITH. Telephone line must be down. We can't
get through. And I shouldn't be surprised if we're
snowed in.

(FRED *whistles.*)

HELEN (*laughing*). Now don't you wish you were
back in Cannes ?

FRED. That's right, Miss Tennant. Bitter cold up

in the store-room, and the bar too. Been wearing my
overcoat. Can't we have the heat on up there, Mr.
Henley ?

KEITH. No, Fred, we can't. Plant isn't working.
(*Crossing to* HELEN.) Burton went off this morning to
get some new parts.

(*Enter* SALLY, *followed by* CLARA. FRED *moves to the
door* L.)

SALLY (*lighting up*). Hello, Fred !

FRED. Sally Philips ! Keeping well ?

SALLY. I was before I landed up here. (*To* CLARA,
impressively.) This is Fred.

CLARA (*impressed, to* FRED). Oo, I've heard a lot
about you.

FRED. Well, don't believe all you hear. That's
right, isn't it, Mr. Henley ?

(*He takes out a cigarette in dashing manner, lights it neatly
with a lighter, nods and winks and goes off* L. CLARA
and SALLY *gaze after him in profound admiration, then
slowly go on clearing during the following dialogue.*)

KEITH (*to* HELEN). No, you needn't have come here
so early, you know——

HELEN (*smiling*). That's not very complimentary.

KEITH (*hastily*). Oh—I mean—I'm awfully glad you
did—naturally——

HELEN. Why—naturally ?

KEITH (*warmly, but confusedly*). Well, I mean, I was
looking forward to seeing as much of you as I could.
And your being here is the only bright spot in this show
just now. But I was thinking about *you*. It's beastly
uncomfortable, with just a skeleton staff like this, and
there can't be much for you to do.

HELEN. No, I don't suppose there is, but I was dead
keen to get started, so when they told me at head office
you people were coming up, I thought I'd better come
too and see if my things were going to be all right. As
a matter of fact, I've put in some pretty good work
already—taken notes of what there is and what there
isn't——

KEITH (*enthusiastically*). Good! Give them to me and I'll see you get what you want.

HELEN (*rising and crossing to R. of the table.*) And I've got some rather bright ideas about turning that long lounge into a proper games room.

KEITH (*coming down to her and crossing L. with her*). Just what we want, of course. Look here, I know it's filthily cold along there and you're probably rather tired —but would you like to show me what exactly you'd like to do ?

HELEN. Love to. Wait a minute—where's my notebook ? I feel very grand with my notebook.

KEITH (*escorting her out L.*). You *look* very grand with your notebook.

(*They go out.* SALLY *and* CLARA *stop work at once.*)

CLARA (*whispering urgently*). See the way he looked at 'er. Oo—proper case, I calls it. Make a nice pair, wouldn't they ?

SALLY. Yes, all right.

CLARA (*above the table—slowly folding serviettes*). Oo —I think she's lovely. I think he's lovely too.

SALLY. Go on. I suppose you think everything in the garden's lovely. Sentimental, that's what you are.

CLARA (*innocently*). I know. Aren't you ?

SALLY. No, I've seen too much. It takes a lot to take me in now. (*She pauses—then comes down to* CLARA, *polishing a tumbler.*) What do you think of Fred ?

CLARA. I thought he was lovely too.

SALLY. He's a smart boy, Fred is. Clever. Nice manners with everybody, high or low. Makes a lot o' money too, Fred does.

CLARA (*rather wistfully*). Is he married ?

SALLY. Not that I know of. And if there's been one after him, there's been hundreds. Won't let him alone. Guests too—rich women. I've seen them in his bar.

CLARA (*aghast*). Were they after him too ?

SALLY. Yes. Some of these rich women's worse than we are—and we're bad enough. (*She goes back to the sideboard.*)

CLARA. What does *she* do ?

SALLY. Who ? Miss Tennant ?

CLARA. Yes.

SALLY. She's sort of hostess. She introduces 'em, and asks 'em if they'd like to play tennis or golf or cards.

CLARA. Well, don't they know whether they'd like to play ?

SALLY. No, some of 'em don't know anything. Half barmy. They build these hotels for them people.

CLARA. And is that all she'll do ?

SALLY. Well, she's at it all day and half the night, 'cos she has to ask 'em if they'd like to dance at night —they don't know until she asks 'em—and she has to be polite and smile all the time and say (*with burlesque of* HELEN's *best Mayfair accent*), " Oh yers, of cors, how jally ripping ! " Drive you potty !

(MRS. HEATON *enters* L. *and looks round quickly.*)

MRS. HEATON (*a trifle hesitantly, staying at the door*). Where's Mr. Jordan ?

SALLY (*coolly*). He's along there somewhere (*indicating kitchens*)—drinking himself unconscious.

MRS. HEATON (*angrily*). How dare you ! What do you mean ?

SALLY. Well, that's what he said he was going to do.

(MRS. HEATON *gives her a furious look and then marches off* R. SALLY *and* CLARA *look after her, then look at each other.*)

CLARA (*lowering her voice*). What's matter with her ?

SALLY. Don't ask me. It just shows you. They said she was the nicest staff manageress in the company. My friend was under her at the Bournemouth hotel and said you couldn't wish for anybody nicer.

CLARA. Well, I don't think she's nice.

SALLY. Nice ! If she's like this now, when there's just a few of us here, all being matey like, what's she going to be like when everybody comes and we're run off our feet ? She's going to be murder.

CLARA (*as if this followed*). I think I'd better make some more tea.

Sᴀʟʟʏ. Yes, you do.

(Cʟᴀʀᴀ *goes off* ʀ. Mʀs. Hᴇᴀᴛᴏɴ *comes in* ʀ. *carrying the bottle that* Jᴏʀᴅᴀɴ *went off with. The tissue-paper is torn. She marches straight out* ʟ. *with it, looking determined.* Sᴀʟʟʏ *watches her, then calls.*)

Hoy, Clara. Did you see what she had with her ?
    Cʟᴀʀᴀ (*sticking her head in, confidentially*). I didn't notice. What was it ?
    Sᴀʟʟʏ (*triumphantly, as she folds up the tablecloth*). It was that bottle Mr. Jordan took in there. She's taken it away from him.
    Cʟᴀʀᴀ (*gasping*). But how could she ?
    Sᴀʟʟʏ. Now you're asking. He's big enough to stand up for his own bottle.
    Cʟᴀʀᴀ. She's nothing to do with him, has she ?
    Sᴀʟʟʏ. I didn't know she had. But she can go and take his drink away from him.
    Cʟᴀʀᴀ (*eagerly*). Then she must have something to do with him.

(*As she says this,* Eᴅɴᴀ Sᴀɴᴅᴀʀs *strolls in* ʟ. Cʟᴀʀᴀ's *head disappears.*)

Eᴅɴᴀ. What's the argument ?
    Sᴀʟʟʏ (*approaching with the folded tablecloth and speaking confidentially*). How can Mrs. Heaton go and take Mr. Jordan's bottle away from him ?
    Eᴅɴᴀ (*solemnly*). I give it up, Sally. What's the answer ? (*She sits* ʟ. *of the table.*)
    Sᴀʟʟʏ. Well, that's what we want to know.
    Eᴅɴᴀ. Oh—I thought you'd invented a dirty riddle. Where is everybody ? Where's Keith Henley ?
    Sᴀʟʟʏ. He had a very tender conversation with Miss Tennant, and then they went off to look at one of the lounges. (*She puts the cloth on the sideboard.*)
    Eᴅɴᴀ (*significantly*). Ah, we're all having a very long and busy day, aren't we ?

(Cʟᴀʀᴀ *pops her head in* ʀ.)

CLARA (*excitedly*).   I heard a car.   Round at the back.
SALLY.   Go right through and see.

(CLARA *goes*.)

Clara's a nice girl, but straight out of the egg.   I wonder
who's there.

EDNA.   Probably yesterday's milk.

(JORDAN *enters from* R., *gloomier than ever*.)

JORDAN.   I heard a car.
EDNA.   I've been hearing a lot about it too.
JORDAN (*coming to below* R. *of the table and lowering his
voice*).   Do you know if Fred's up in his store-room ?
EDNA.   I think so.
JORDAN.   Let me see, you were working with—er—
Mrs. Heaton just now.
EDNA.   Yes, but I tore myself away.   I think she's
having fun by herself now with the counterpanes.

(JORDAN *crosses to the door* L. *in front of* EDNA.)

Want to see her ?
JORDAN (*in a tiny whisper*).   No.   Fred.

(*He goes out* R.   EDNA *and* SALLY *look at each other*.)

EDNA.   Yes, you're right.   There's a mystery there
SALLY.   You see——
EDNA.   Yes, I remember.   Why did she take his
bottle away ?   I still don't know.

(CLARA *enters* R., *all a-goggle, followed by* CROWTHER,
*dressed in heavy overcoat, still wet from snowflakes, and
shaking his hat.* CLARA *stays at the door*.)

CLARA.   It's Mr. Crowther.
EDNA (*recognizing him*).   Not our own detective ?
It is.   Nice work, Mr. Crowther.   I knew somebody
would find us.   What did you use—bloodhounds ?
CROWTHER (R. *of the table*).   I think I've heard this
funny line before, haven't I ?
EDNA (*rising and coming round to front of the table and
speaking in same burlesque " bright " manner*).   Yes, Mr.
Crowther.   Sandars is the name, Edna Sandars.

CROWTHER (*without enthusiasm*). I remember.

EDNA (*same manner*). Yes, the last time we met was last autumn at our Bournemouth establishment. You wanted thirty-five bob for expenses from the till and I wouldn't let you have it without a note from head office. We had quite an argument——

CROWTHER (*cutting in, heavily*). All right, all right. (*To* CLARA.) Mr. Henley's here, isn't he ? Well, tell him *I'm* here.

SALLY. I'll tell him.

EDNA. No, let me. I'll enjoy it more than you.

(*She goes out quickly* L. CROWTHER *is now taking off his overcoat.*)

CROWTHER (*to* CLARA, *who is staring at him*). What's your name ?

CLARA. Clara Packer.

CROWTHER. Well, Miss Clara Packer, if you'd take this hat and coat and put 'em where they might dry, and then bring me a nice hot cup of tea, I'd be obliged.

CLARA (*taking his hat and coat*). I was just making some tea.

CROWTHER. That's a good girl.

(CLARA *takes things out* R. SALLY *follows to the door* R. *with the tray.* CROWTHER *notices her.*)

Hello, I've met you before. Where was it ?

SALLY (*sulkily*). London.

CROWTHER. You mean at our London hotel ?

(SALLY *nods sulkily.*)

Yes—now wait a minute. You—— (*He rubs his chin, looking at her.*)

SALLY (*bitterly*). Yes, I was one of the five chamber-maids you put in a row and accused of stealing a fur coat——

CROWTHER. Ah—that was it, yes. The fur-coat job.

SALLY (*indignantly, her back to the open door*). Yes, and though I'd never set eyes on the coat and hadn't looked after the woman who said she'd lost it, you put

me through it with the other four, and after that everybody in the place looked sideways at me.

CROWTHER (*ignoring this outburst*). Let's see—what
was *your* name ?

SALLY (*at the door, impudently*). You'll be surprised.
Greta Garbo.

(*She exits. CROWTHER looks at the door and nods his
head solemnly, as if saying to himself, " You look out,
my girl." He has just finished doing this, when* KEITH
HENLEY, *looking astonished, enters quickly* L.)

KEITH. Crowther ! What on earth are you doing
here ?

CROWTHER (*with a rueful grin*). Trying to find the
North Pole. That's what it feels like. But head office
told me to go round and see you all, on a special job.

KEITH. Yes, but we're not open, you know. Staff's
not here yet. Only a few of us, taking stock, and so on.
The rest of 'em won't be here for another week.

CROWTHER. Oh, I know that. But I want to know
exactly who is here.

KEITH. All right, but what's the idea ?

CROWTHER (*seriously*). Can't tell you that, yet. But
it's a serious job. They don't send me out like this for
fun, y'know. Can we talk here ?

KEITH. Yes. Sit down.

(*He indicates the two chairs* R. CROWTHER *takes the lower
one,* KEITH *the other.*)

It's about as good as anywhere. Better, because at
least it's warm. You see, the big plant's broken down.
Burton, the engineer, went off this morning. We're in
a mess here, Crowther.   Latest news is that the telephone
line must be down. Can't get through to the exchange.
Jolly, isn't it ?

CROWTHER. Yes, and it may be worse before it's
better. It's still snowing like the devil, and it took me
all my time to get my little car through at all. Wouldn't
surprise me if we're not snowed up in a few hours' time.

(*Enter* CLARA R. *with a cup of tea, which she puts on the upstage* R. *corner of the table, then fetches the sugar-basin from the sideboard.*)

Ah—thanks—just what I wanted.

CLARA (*languishingly to* KEITH). Wouldn't you like one, Mr. Henley ?

KEITH. No, thank you, Clara. But keep the kettle going. And clean up in there.

CLARA. Yes, sir. (*She crosses to the door* R.)

CROWTHER. That's right. We don't want to be disturbed for a few minutes—see ?

(CLARA *nods and goes out* R., *shutting the door behind her.* CROWTHER *crosses to the table and picks up the tea, then perches on the corner of the table, facing* KEITH. *The latter rises.*)

KEITH. You want to know who's here *now*, eh ?

CROWTHER (*takes a sip of tea, then produces a notebook*). Yes, I want to know who's here—and why ?

KEITH (*confidentially*). Right. But first, I ought to explain we're making a big push here this season. Last week, at head office, the Chief told me they think they can make this an English *Gleneagles*. We're having Chick Blaze's Band—which'll cost 'em two hundred and fifty a week—right through from June to September. And though they've kept me on as assistant manager—thank God !—they're moving in some of the best people we've got in nearly all the departments. So we're all on our toes. (*During the following* KEITH *moves down stage* R. *and back occasionally while* CROWTHER *jots down his notes.*) But you want to know who's here now. Well, there's Arnold Jordan who'll be chief assistant chef under old Marini. He's been reporting on the kitchens—with Burton to explain the plant. You know Arnold, don't you ?

CROWTHER. Yes, I think so. Frenchman, isn't he ?

KEITH. I believe he's only half-French. Nice chap. Bit gloomy, just now.

CROWTHER. What's he gloomy about ?

KEITH. I dunno. Perhaps the weather's getting him

down. He doesn't like the kitchens either. Then there's Miss Tennant—Helen Tennant. She's sports and social hostess.

CROWTHER. What's she doing here already ?

KEITH. Oh—well—this is her first big job—she was assistant before—and she wanted to look round and make suggestions in good time. She's very keen, y'know, not like some of the girls we've had. Just the right type.

CROWTHER. Was she down at Cannes part of the time last year ?

KEITH. Yes. Know her ?

CROWTHER (*making a note*). I think so. Next ?

KEITH. Mrs. Heaton. She's going to be staff manageress, but she's doing housekeeper's work just now. Very hard worker, doesn't say much for herself. She's new to me, but you may have struck her.

CROWTHER (*making a note*). Yes, I remember her.

KEITH. Then Fred's here—you know, in the cocktail bar.

CROWTHER. Oh—he's going to be up here, is he ? But what's *he* come so soon for ?

KEITH. He's only come for a couple of days, to take stock and look the bar over. He says head office never get him all the various fancy drinks he needs in time, so he'd come and then ginger them up. The cocktail bar here should be worth a lot this season.

CROWTHER (*making a note*). He was down at Cannes last season too, wasn't he ? Then there's this cheeky girl—what's her name—Sandars ? I suppose she's bookkeeping ?

KEITH. Yes, she'll be up here this season. They sent her in advance to help us with stock and letters. She's a secretary as well as a bookkeeper.

CROWTHER (*making a note*). She's got a lot o' lip. Always had.

KEITH. Yes, I've had to pull her up once or twice already. She's been rude to Miss Tennant, who's been very decent about it, considering she's not used to that kind of thing.

CROWTHER. Are these two the only maids they've sent up so far?

KEITH. Sally and Clara? Yes. Just to look after us, and help Mrs. Heaton. Don't know much about them.

CROWTHER (*closing the notebook*). Oh—I can attend to them. I know their sort, and I've had dealings with one of 'em already. And that's the lot?

KEITH. Yes.

CROWTHER (*finishing his tea*). Right. Now don't mention to anybody I've come round on a special job. If they want to know, just tell 'em I've dropped in.

(KEITH *nods, and goes to the door* R. *to call one of the maids.*)

KEITH. Oh—Sally—Clara—one of you. Tell Mrs. Heaton that Mr. Crowther's here and he'll want a bedroom.

CROWTHER. I'd like a warm one.

KEITH (*grinning*). You're out of luck.

(CLARA *goes through to the door* L. *and out.*)

Your car all right?

CROWTHER. Should be. I ran it right under the back entrance—you know that space there? Seemed warm enough under there.

KEITH. Yes, that's where I keep mine. And Miss Tennant's got hers there.

(*Enter* JORDAN L. *He is surprised to see* CROWTHER. *He crosses* R. *above the table.*)

JORDAN. Hello! I didn't expect to see you here, Mr. Crowther.

CROWTHER. No, I ran in for a cheap night's lodging. How are you, Mr. Jordan?

JORDAN. Not so good, not so good. (*He brings* CROWTHER *down* R.) Now—tell me—you have been a policeman——

CROWTHER. I was nearly twenty years at Scotland Yard, if that's what you mean by being a policeman——

JORDAN. Yes, it is. Well, then, tell me something.

Is there a nice big prison in a warmer place than this ?
Not Dartmoor, that must be as bad as this.

(KEITH *crosses* C. *up stage, sits on the table and watches
these two with amusement.*)

CROWTHER. Well, there's Parkhurst, in the Isle of
Wight.

JORDAN. That's the place. Now, supposing I com-
mit a crime, and I am found out, would they send me
to Parkhurst ?

CROWTHER. Why, would you like to try your hand
at something ?

JORDAN. Yes. Something with plenty of money in
it. If it comes off, I go at once to the South of France
or the Argentine. If I am found out, they send me to
Parkhurst in the Isle of Wight. And that will be better
than staying here.

CROWTHER. The food wouldn't be as good.

JORDAN. Food ! I hate food ! Besides—once in
prison, perhaps they would make me chef. I think I
should like to cook for convicts for a change. I am tired
of the rich. I am tired of trying to tickle their fat
stomachs.

KEITH. Hoy, don't you start going Bolshie, Arnold !

(*Enter* HELEN TENNANT L., *looking animated. She crosses*
R.C. *below the table, putting her handbag on the bottom
left-hand corner as she passes.*)

JORDAN. Miss Tennant, you are looking very, very
pretty. (*He kisses his hand to her and moves up* R.)

HELEN. How nice ! That's probably because I've
just been having a row.

KEITH. You've probably met Mr. Crowther before,
haven't you ? He's the company's detective.

HELEN (*smiling*). Yes, I think I have. How d'you
do ?

(CROWTHER *greets her* R. KEITH *drops down* L. *of her.*)

CROWTHER. How d'*you* do, Miss Tennant ? And
who've you been having a row with ?

HELEN (*more to* KEITH). After you left, the Sandars girl really was the limit. She seemed to think—just because I'd ignored her bits of rudeness, so far—she could say what she liked. So she started again, and I flared up and jolly well ticked her off.

KEITH. Quite right.

CROWTHER. Yes, I'm all for that piece getting it in the neck. Too cheeky by half.

(FRED *looks in at the door* L.)

FRED (*brightly*). Hello, Mr. Crowther. Just heard you'd arrived.

CROWTHER. Came in out of the snow, Fred. (*He crosses* C. *below the table and shakes hands with* FRED, *while* JORDAN *joins* KEITH *and* HELEN.) How are you ?

FRED. Might be worse. Thought about turning in soon. I've had a long day, checking up on everything.

CROWTHER. Saw an old friend of yours in town, the other day, Fred. Charlie.

FRED. What, Charlie Francis ?

CROWTHER. No, have another guess. Anyhow, they were just sending him up for two years.

FRED. Couldn't have been an old friend of mine, then, Mr. Crowther.

CROWTHER. Perhaps not, but you know him.

FRED (*with mock disgust*). I have to know too many people. That's what's wrong with my little job. Can't afford to be particular. If you're going to be taken bad in the night, Mr. Crowther, I *might* be able to find something that 'ud take the pain away. And my room's Number Twenty-Seven. Nighty-night, all.

THE OTHERS (*variously*). 'Night. Good night, Fred. Be good. (*Etc.*)

(FRED *withdraws* L.)

KEITH (*to* CROWTHER). What about some food ?

(*On the word* " food," JORDAN *slowly and furtively crosses* HELEN *and makes for the door* R.)

CROWTHER. Well, I had a sort of late high tea on the

way. But I wouldn't mind a sandwich or two before I turn in. Unless Mr. Jordan here would like to make me something tasty and dainty.

JORDAN (*turning at the door and crossing to* CROWTHER, *who is* C.). Tasty and dainty ! Mr. Crowther, you have been reading the woman's page in the newspaper. How to make a tasty, dainty dish—for tuppence ha'penny—for your poor long-suffering idiot of a husband ! (*Moving to the door* R.) You'll have sandwiches, and they won't be either tasty or dainty.

(*He goes out* R.)

HELEN (*dropping her voice, to* KEITH). Is he always like that ?

KEITH. I don't know, but nearly all chefs are nearly always like that.

CROWTHER (*heartily*). Either bad-tempered or miserable, most of 'em. They say it's the heat o' the kitchens does it. Don't enjoy their food neither.

(*Enter* MRS. HEATON L. *She nods to* CROWTHER.)

MRS. HEATON. I'll show you where your room is, Mr. Crowther.

CROWTHER. Right. Thanks. I've a bag. Must have left it out there somewhere.

(*He goes out* R., *leaving the door open behind him.*)

MRS. HEATON. It's still snowing hard, Mr. Henley. Do you think they'll have the telephone line all right in the morning ?

KEITH. I shouldn't think so. There's a lot of wire between us and the exchange and they won't be able to do much with the job in this weather.

MRS. HEATON (*in cheerless tone*). No, I suppose not. (*She moves down to the notice-board.*)

HELEN. You sound awfully depressed about it, Mrs. Heaton. Cheer up !

MRS. HEATON (*rather coolly*). I'm sorry, but I don't feel very cheerful.

KEITH. You're as bad as Arnold Jordan. He's in the dumps too.

Mrs. Heaton (*coolly*). Is he ? I'm very glad to hear it.

Helen (*reproachfully*). Oh—Mrs. Heaton. Don't be mean.

Mrs. Heaton (*coolly*). I'm not mean.

(Clara *looks in* l., *gasping with excitement*.)

Clara. Here—— (*Gasping.*)

(*They stare at her.*)

Keith (*humorously*). Where ?

Clara. There's somebody ringing at the front door. Ringing and ringing.

(Crowther *enters from* r., *carrying a small suitcase.*)

Crowther. What's this ?

Keith. Somebody trying to get in.

Crowther. Better tell 'em they're a fortnight too early.

Keith. Just give 'em a shout—no, I'll go.

(*He goes out* l. *and* Clara *withdraws with him.*)

Mrs. Heaton (*to* Crowther). Shall I show you where your room is now ?

Crowther (*up stage, putting the suitcase on a chair by the sideboard*). Just a minute. I'd like to see who's doing the ringing.

Helen. You're very suspicious, Mr. Crowther.

Crowther. No, I'm not, Miss Tennant. I'm just curious, that's all.

Helen. You haven't *really* told us what you're doing here yet.

Crowther. Yes, I have. I've come in out of the snow.

(Helen *sits* r. *and starts to read. Enter* Edna Sandars l., *wearing horn-rimmed spectacles on the end of her nose and smoking a cigarette.*)

Edna. Well, I've got some nice long letters ready for head office. (*She puts her things on the sideboard.*) All we want now is Santa Claus and some reindeer to go and post 'em.

CROWTHER (*with heavy irony*). It must be a treat for everybody having you here—being funny all the time.

EDNA (*shaking her head at him*). Mr. Crowther, you can do better than that. You did when you couldn't get that thirty-five bob out of me at Bournemouth. (*She crosses in front of* CROWTHER *to* R. *end of the table, on which she sits, facing* HELEN.)

(MRS. HEATON *is still studying the notice-board.*)

(*With mock sweetness, to* HELEN.) I hope you're not feeling too tired, Miss Tennant, after your first long day here.

HELEN (*coldly*). No, I'm not. Are you ?

EDNA (*coolly*). Yes. And one foot's gone already with frostbite.

MRS. HEATON (*suddenly, and very crossly*). Oh—be quiet !

EDNA (*standing up and turning to her—astonished by this outburst*). What ?

MRS. HEATON (*fiercely*). I said, " Be quiet." You get on my nerves. Things are bad enough——

EDNA (*quietly*). What things, Mrs. Heaton ?

(MRS. HEATON *does not reply.*)

All right. You win.

(*A pause.* CLARA *enters* L., *followed by* KEITH, *who closes the door.* CLARA *goes straight across and goes out* R., *leaving the door open.*)

KEITH. Nobody there now.

EDNA (*crossing back to the sideboard* L.C.). Nobody where ?

KEITH. There was somebody ringing at the front. I'm sorry for the poor blighters if they thought the hotel was open. But that's not likely. Nobody would climb to the top of this hill in a snowstorm just to see if the Greenfingers Palace Hotel was open. (*Dropping down* L.)

MRS. HEATON. Perhaps they've gone round to the back.

KEITH. It's possible.

(*He glances towards the door* R. *At this moment, voices—*
SALLY'S *and* MISS TRACEY'S—*are heard off* R. *Both are
talking at once and no words can be distinguished.
Everybody listens and looks. Then* MISS TRACEY *dashes
in, followed hard by* SALLY. MISS TRACEY *is well
wrapped up in thick tweed coat, etc.*)

MISS TRACEY (*crossing to bottom* R. *corner of the table*).
Good evening, everybody. Isn't this fun ?

SALLY (*at the door*). I couldn't stop her. She would
come in.

MISS TRACEY. I should think not, indeed ! Who's
in charge here ?

KEITH. Well, I suppose I am——

MISS TRACEY. How d'you do ? My name's Tracey,
Miss Tracey. You'll have to put me up for the night,
y'know.

KEITH (*apologetically*). But the hotel's not open.
It's not even ready to open.

MISS TRACEY. Very stupid of me, of course.

(CROWTHER *drifts down* R. *of* MISS TRACEY.)

But I couldn't possibly go anywhere else now. The
snow's so thick. My little car wouldn't get through.
(*To* CROWTHER.) Hello, I've seen you before, I think,
haven't I ?

CROWTHER (*not too graciously*). I believe I've seen
you too.

KEITH. This is Mr. Crowther, one of our company
officials.

MISS TRACEY (*pointing to him, triumphantly*). You're
the hotel company's detective, aren't you. (*To the
company in general.*) Isn't this exciting ? (*To* KEITH.)
By the way, Mr.——

KEITH. Henley's my name. (*Crossing* C.) I'm the
assistant manager of this hotel.

MISS TRACEY. And very nice for you, Mr. Henley.
I was just going to say that I happen to be a shareholder
in this company, and I'm also very well acquainted with

your chairman of directors, Sir Richard Parks. If that
helps.

KEITH.   It does, rather, Miss Tracey.

MISS TRACEY.   So I can stay!

KEITH.   Yes, so long as you understand that we're
not open, that there are just a few of us camping here
and it won't be comfortable, we can certainly give you
a night's shelter.

MISS TRACEY.   Thank you. Oh—there are two of
us, y'know. I have a companion out in the car. She's
asleep, poor dear, and very well wrapped up with a hot-
water bottle, so I thought I wouldn't worry until everything was ready.

KEITH.   I see. You'll want two rooms, then.

MISS TRACEY.   If we could have two connecting
rooms, that would be splendid.

KEITH (*after thinking a moment, going to* MRS. HEATON).
Mrs. Heaton, I think the best thing would be to use the
manager's suite. That's got two good connecting rooms,
and I know they're warm and dry. You know them—
right at the end?

MRS. HEATON.   Yes. (*To* MISS TRACEY.) I'll show
them to you.

MISS TRACEY.   Thank you.

CROWTHER.   And you can show me where I'm sleeping
at the same time, Mrs. Heaton.

MRS. HEATON.   Yes. Sally. Clara. I shall want
you too.

(*She goes off* L., *followed by* MISS TRACEY, CROWTHER
carrying his bag, SALLY *and* CLARA *carrying* MISS
TRACEY'S *bag. This leaves* KEITH, HELEN *and* EDNA
on the stage. KEITH L., HELEN R. *and* EDNA *up*
C.)

EDNA (*coming down* C. *and sitting on the table facing*
L.).   Gosh!

KEITH.   Extraordinary old girl, charging in here like
that!

HELEN.   Probably a bit potty, but quite definitely a
lady.

KEITH. Yes, and obviously I couldn't turn her out, a night like this.

EDNA (*dryly*). Especially if she really *is* a friend of the chairman.

KEITH. I don't think that's a bluff. An ordinary member of the public wouldn't know Sir Richard was our chairman.

EDNA. We'll have to be on our best behaviour.

HELEN (*rising, crossing* L. *above the table and not noticing her handbag which is on lower* L. *corner of the table*). Well, I'll make a beginning by going to bed. (*Smiling at* KEITH.) I really am tired now.

KEITH (*very sympathetically*). You must be. Never mind, you've done a jolly good day's work for the pub. Can you find your way up all right ?

(*He is now moving with her to the door* L. EDNA *watches them both, and as* KEITH *ceremoniously opens the door for* HELEN, *speaks.*)

EDNA (*rather unctuously*). Go-oo-od night, Miss Tennant.

(*This is ignored. The two go out. As soon as they have gone,* EDNA, *suddenly alert, leans over the table and takes up the bag. She gives a sharp glance at the door* L., *listens a moment, then opens the bag. She has only time to take one peep into the bag before the door* L. *opens quickly. She is able to shut the bag, that is all, before* HELEN *is back.*)

HELEN (*sharply*). That's my bag.

EDNA (*with innocent stare*). Oh—is it ? I was just admiring it.

(HELEN *holds out her hand for it, and* EDNA *hands it over. The two girls look at each other for a moment, obvious antagonists. Both are above the table.*)

HELEN (*softly*). I'm afraid you're not only very bad-mannered, Miss Sandars, but you're also a bit of a liar.

EDNA (*coolly*). Better call me a thief too, while you're at it.

HELEN.   No, I've no evidence for that—yet.

(*She turns and goes, leaving the door* L. *open behind her. Her voice and* KEITH'S *are heard through it.* EDNA *stands and listens.*)

(*Off.*) Yes, I've got it.   No, I can find my way up, thanks.   Good night.

KEITH (*off, unctuously*).   Good night, Miss Tennant.

EDNA (*irritated, muttering*).   Er-t-cher !   (*She moves away* R.)

(KEITH *returns, closing the door.   He looks at* EDNA *as if he were annoyed with her.*)

(*Coming to* R. *end of the table.*)   Well—say it.

KEITH (*at* L. *end of the table*).   I think I'd better.

EDNA.   All right.   But just a minute.   Is this official or not ?   It's getting late, and I think it's about time we were off duty.

KEITH.   What difference does that make ?

EDNA.   A lot.   It's the difference between the assist-ant manager talking to one of his female slaves, and Keith Henley talking to Edna Sandars.

KEITH.   All right.   This is a bit of both.

EDNA.   That's not good enough.   Come on, be a man.   It's late.   If you want to tick me off, make it personal, so I can answer back.

KEITH (*with more heat*).   It's time you did some listen-ing, never mind answering back.

EDNA.   Well, speak your piece.   Then I'll say mine.

(*But they are interrupted by* MISS TRACEY, *who enters* L. *She is no longer wearing her hat and thick coat.   She is in high spirits.*)

MISS TRACEY (*coming down* L.).   Well, I must say it all looks very nice, as well as being the most gratifying adventure.   Two very pleasant communicating rooms.

KEITH.   Good !   Now what about the other lady ?

MISS TRACEY.   My companion ?   Yes, that's why I came down.   She's very tired—poor thing—and nearly as deaf as a post—and probably she won't wake up properly.

(EDNA *sits on* R. *edge of the table.*)

Now I thought I'd slip back and see that her room was all ready for her, so that she can hop straight into bed. If you give me about ten minutes, and then send one of those maids out to the car to bring her in—I've told them where the car is—just outside, but under cover— you know the place—then we'll be all settled and no time wasted. Is that clear ?

KEITH. Yes. But I can bring her in.

MISS TRACEY (*crossing* C. *below the table*). I know you could—and it's very nice of you to suggest it—but I really think it would be better if one of the maids did it. The poor old thing might wonder what was happening if she suddenly saw a strange young man. In about five or ten minutes, eh ?

KEITH (*glancing at his watch*). All right, Miss Tracey. I'll send one of them along for her. She can bring her bag too.

MISS TRACEY. Just what I was about to suggest. I can see you're cut out for this business. I must tell Sir Richard so. Your housekeeper or manageress or whatever she is——

KEITH. Mrs. Heaton.

MISS TRACEY. Mrs. Heaton, yes. She's a nice woman, but rather unhappy at present—poor thing— she's got something unpleasant on her mind. (*To* KEITH.) Have you noticed that ?

EDNA (*coolly*). Yes.

MISS TRACEY (*taking her in*). I dare say you have. You look a sharp young woman. Well, now, I'll go upstairs again. (*Moves towards the door* R., *not* L.) Could I possibly go through this way ? I like to know my way about when I'm staying anywhere.

KEITH (*opening the door* R. *for her*). Yes, you can go through there, then turn to the right and up the stairs— if you prefer that way.

MISS TRACEY. I think I do. It makes it all the more

amusing. This may be all very dull to you, but I assure you it's quite an adventure to me. Empty hotel, snowstorm, miles from anywhere—*most* amusing and romantic, I call it. *And* a detective staying here, to look after us. Well, now—I don't know that I shall be coming down again——

KEITH (*smiling*). We're all on our way to bed, I think.

MISS TRACEY. I'm sure you must be. So—good night. Thank you so much. Good night.

KEITH
EDNA }(*together*). Good night.

(She goes. KEITH *closes the door after her, then comes back up* R.)

EDNA. Complicated old party, isn't she—rather?

KEITH (*indifferently*). Oh—I don't know. They're always rather fussy, these elderly spinsters who travel round. Seen hundreds of 'em.

EDNA. So have I. I've had a few years in this business too, y'know. But that's not the ordinary type of fusser—oh, no!

KEITH. Bit more enterprising and eccentric perhaps, that's all.

EDNA (*satirically*). All right, Mr. Henley. You know it all.

KEITH (*rather fiercely*). I know this——

EDNA (*cutting in*). Now we're for it.

KEITH (*angrily*). You're going to get yourself into trouble—and quite soon—if you don't stop being rude to Miss Tennant——

EDNA. Yes, yes, I thought so.

KEITH (*same tone*). Miss Tennant has one of the most important and difficult jobs in this hotel. It's not easy for a girl of her class to come and earn her living as she's doing. I respect and admire her for it. I like the way she's so keen, too, and I believe she's going to be a success here.

EDNA. In fact, she's all super-de-luxe. I know.

KEITH. I'm afraid with you it's just a case of plain jealousy.

EDNA (*surprisingly, quite serious*). You may be quite right. I hate to think it, but you may be. Probably I *am* jealous.

KEITH. Perhaps I ought to have said envious.

EDNA. No, jealous is better.

KEITH. Well, whatever it is you feel, just keep it to yourself in future. If you don't, there's going to be a row. And that's both official and personal, Miss Edna Sandars.

EDNA. Well, Mr. Henley, it's late and I consider myself off duty. So now *I'll* be personal. I'd heard a lot of nice things about you, and I think most of them are true. I don't like most of the men I've met in this business, and I've had nearly ten years of it. But I like you. And because I like you, I'm going to warn you that if you're not careful, you'll make a fool of yourself.

KEITH (*half amused, half angry*). Well, of all the damned cheek! I'm glad you said you were going to be personal.

EDNA. Are you going to be grand about this?

KEITH. Not too grand, I hope.

EDNA. Well, then, I'm serious. Be very careful. (*She suddenly produces a smile.*) Please!

KEITH. You may know what you're talking about, but I don't. You'd better explain.

EDNA (*decidedly*). No. Can't be done. You've said your piece. I've said mine.

KEITH. Yes, but you understood mine. I can't make head or tail of yours.

EDNA (*enigmatically*). Then that's your bad luck—or mine. (*She moves away down* C., *then* L.)

(MRS. HEATON *enters* L. *followed by* SALLY *and* CLARA, *who cross to the door* R.)

KEITH. Oh—one of you girls must go in a minute or two to get out the old lady out of the car at the back.

MRS. HEATON. Yes, Mr. Henley. Clara's going.

KEITH. And bring her bag, Clara, if it's not too heavy for you.

CLARA (*just going out* R.). Yes, Mr. Henley.

(*She and* SALLY *go off* R.)

MRS. HEATON. They'll be all right in there, Mr. Henley. (*She sits* C. *above the table and begins to look through her notebook.*)

KEITH (*yawning slightly*). I feel like turning in.

EDNA (*sitting in the chair* L. *of the table*). I'm going—as soon as I've seen Visitor Number Two.

KEITH (*sitting* R. *by the small table*). Why wait for her ? I have to, but you needn't.

EDNA. Because I'm curious. I never like to miss anything.

MRS. HEATON (*looking up, calmly*). Doesn't it ever get you into trouble ?

EDNA (*with equal calm*). Yes—often. But I'd rather be in trouble—at least *most* kinds of trouble—than be bored.

(*Enter* JORDAN *from* R.)

KEITH. Hello, Arnold, I thought you'd gone to bed.

JORDAN (*moving up* R.C., *with a quick side-glance at* MRS. HEATON, *then turning and addressing* KEITH). No, I have been working—and brooding—in the kitchen. I have written part of a report too—very hot and strong—but I did not finish it.

EDNA. What's the use ? There'll be no post leaving here in the morning.

KEITH. Why ?

EDNA. We'll be snowed up.

JORDAN. I was thinking too. We advertise this expensive dance band. But we do not advertise what chefs we have. Yet the chefs in an hotel can give more pleasure to the guests than any dance band. The company does not announce : " Alberto Marini, Arnold Jordan, Pierre Videl, Jacob Flusser, will be in the kitchens·of this hotel all the season." If they did, nobody would care. But a dance band—yes, that is big business !

KEITH. The wireless has helped to do that.

JORDAN. If they put me on the wireless, I could save

the stomachs of millions from tinned stuff and ruin. (*He goes up to* R. *end of the sideboard.*)

MRS. HEATON (*calmly*). Yes, but who'd want to listen to *you*?

EDNA (*looking at her sharply*). Here—— (*Stops.*)

MRS. HEATON. Well?

EDNA. It doesn't matter.

(KEITH *has gone to the door* R. *and is looking off.*)

KEITH (*through doorway*). Oh—Clara—if that bag's heavy, don't bother with it.

CLARA (*just off*). No, it's all right, Mr. Henley.

(EDNA *and* MRS. HEATON *rise. They all look at the door and clear a way through from that to the door* L. CLARA *enters, carrying a fairly small old case with one hand, and with the other lightly guiding a small, heavily wrapped-up figure. This elderly lady is rather smaller than* MISS TRACEY. *She is wearing an oldish, full fur coat, almost down to her feet. The large collar is turned up, and her hat is tied round with a scarf, and nothing can be seen of her face but a pair of spectacles she is wearing. Rather uncertainly she makes her way, assisted by* CLARA, *across in front of the table to the door* L., *which is held open for them by* JORDAN. *They go out, and* JORDAN *closes the door.*)

EDNA (*who has been closely watching this progress*). Well, that was that. And now little Edna can call it a day. No, don't trouble to see me to my room, Mr. Henley.

KEITH (*indignantly*). I wasn't going to.

EDNA. 'Night, all.

(*She goes out* L.)

JORDAN (*thoughtfully, moving down* L. *to the notice-board*). I am not sure yet whether I like that girl or I cannot stand her.

MRS. HEATON (*calmly*). It must be terrible for her while you're making your mind up.

KEITH (*stifling a yawn*). It's not very late—in fact

this'll seem early here in a few weeks' time—but I feel
as if it's two in the morning.

MRS. HEATON. That's because it's rather stuffy, with
all the windows closed against the snow.

KEITH (*still struggling with yawns, crossing up stage*).
Ye-es, well—if nobody wants me for anything—I think
I'll turn in. Good night.

MRS. HEATON } (*together*). Good night.
JORDAN

(*He goes out* L. *They are silent for a moment, then* JORDAN
turns and moves to L. *of the table. They both begin
talking angrily and loudly at once, with rather startling
effect.*)

MRS. HEATON		What have you been doing all the evening, that's what I'd like to know, and if you'd wanted to see me why couldn't you have found me upstairs ?
JORDAN	(*together*).	What did you mean by saying, " Who'd want to listen to *me*," in that tone of voice, making me look a fool and also giving the game away ?

(*They both stop short at exactly the same time, glaring at
each other.*)

MRS. HEATON (*after a pause—angrily*). What ?
JORDAN. Eh ?
MRS. HEATON. Don't be idiotic.
JORDAN (*angrily*). Idiotic ! Do you think this is a
little game I play, eh ? I am having fun, eh ? I amuse
myself, eh ?
MRS. HEATON (*suddenly changing her tune*). You
amuse me.
JORDAN (*wildly, turning away* L.). Well, that is
something. I amuse you. Good ! I am delighted.

MRS. HEATON (*calmly*). If you hadn't been hiding out of the way most of the evening, we might have had a sensible talk. Now it's too late.

JORDAN (*wildly—up* L.C., *slightly above* MRS. HEATON). But here we are. At last. By ourselves. In a warm room, too. And now, of course, you say, "No, it is too late."

MRS. HEATON (*calmly*). So it is, for sitting down here. You should have thought of it earlier. And don't try coming into my room. Somebody might see you. Besides, I don't want any more of this ridiculous talk. So please don't try it. (*She pushes her chair in.*)

JORDAN (*sulkily*). How can I try it when I don't even know the number of your room ?

MRS. HEATON (*crossing to the door* L. *in front of* JORDAN). I thought you knew I was given Fifteen——

JORDAN (*eagerly*). Ah—Fifteen, Rose—thank you !

MRS. HEATON. But then I changed it. Good night, Arnold.

(*She goes quickly.*)

JORDAN (*furiously, moving to the door after her*). Then what is it now, you torment of a woman ?

(*He looks out after her, but feels she has gone too far, so, furious, bangs the door and returns.* SALLY *comes in* R. *and moves up* C.)

SALLY. Here, Mr. Jordan, what's on ?

JORDAN (*coming back*). Everything ! I am so angry with that woman. I'll show her. (*Crossing to* SALLY.) What would you say if I kissed you ?

SALLY (*promptly*). Nothing.

(*He gives her a good kiss.*)

Go on.

JORDAN. No, no, Clara my dear——

SALLY. Sally your dear——

JORDAN. Sally my dear, that is enough. And thank you very much.

(CLARA *enters* L.)

SALLY. This is Clara. You see, we're not alike.

CLARA. Who says we are?

SALLY. Nobody. I've made some sandwiches. Would you like a sandwich, Mr. Jordan?

JORDAN. No, I hate sandwiches. Everybody in this barbarian country must eat sandwiches all the time. *And* bacon and eggs! *And* custard! Custard! The whole country is drowned in custard. Good night.

(*He exits* L.)

SALLY (*tenderly*). Good night, Mr. Jordan.

CLARA (*indifferently*). 'Night.

(*The girls giggle.* CLARA *turns eagerly up to* SALLY.)

After I took that old lady into her room, I saw Fred on the landing, and he spoke to me. He *is* nice, isn't he?

SALLY. What did he say?

CLARA. He said, " Good night." But he said it so nicely. I think I'll have a sandwich.

(*She goes off* R., *but leaves the door open.*)

SALLY. Don't you like Mr. Jordan? I do. I've always liked that sort of man. Some size to him. I never did fancy skinny men. When I was at the Majestic that time, there was a waiter on my floor wouldn't leave me alone, but I couldn't bear him. He was like a skeleton. I'll swear you could hear his bones rattling on the corridor.

(CLARA *drifts in, sandwich in hand and her mouth full.*)

He wasn't bad-looking, and he was a smart waiter, but I couldn't fancy him.

CLARA (*her mouth full*). Fancy who?

SALLY (*impatiently*). This chap I'm telling you about.

CLARA (*innocently*). I didn't hear you.

SALLY. You must have got your ears full as well as your mouth. Well, I'm going to bed. (*She turns and sees the door* L. *slowly opening, and looks at it with lively expectation.*) In a minute.

(CROWTHER, *carrying a newspaper and a flask, and now wearing slippers, comes in.* SALLY's *face falls.*)

Oh Lord !—I'd forgotten about you.

CROWTHER (*heartily*).   Ah—that's just where some of you make your mistake—forgetting about me.   (*Noticing* CLARA'S *sandwich.*)   That's what I came down for.   A bite to eat.   Just bring me one or two of them and a glass with a drop of water in, will you ?

(CLARA *nods and goes out* R.)

SALLY (*moving* L.).   Well, now I *am* going to bed.

CROWTHER (*sitting down* L. *of the table*).   And—I dare say—a nice fur coat on it to keep you warm.

SALLY (*angrily, coming back to above him*).   Now don't you start your fur coat stuff with me all over again.   You'd no right to drag me in the last time, and —seeing you made such a fool of yourself—I'd have thought you'd have had sense to shut up about it.

CROWTHER (*complacently*).   You forget I got that coat back.   Give me time, I catch 'em.

SALLY (*going to the door* L.).   About all you'll ever catch is a cold.

(*She goes out.*   CROWTHER *opens his newspaper, a London evening paper.*   CLARA *enters with small tray on which are a plate of sandwiches, a little jug of water and a glass.*)

CROWTHER (*looking up*).   Thank you, young woman.

(*When she puts down the tray, he takes a sandwich and bites at it, then pours some whisky from his flask into the glass and adds some water, talking while doing this.*)

Let's see, what's your name ?   Alice ?

CLARA.   No, Clara.

CROWTHER.   New to this, aren't you ?

CLARA.   Yes.   I've just started.

CROWTHER.   Well, just watch your step, Clara my girl.   Don't try to be one of the clever ones.   Too many of 'em in the hotel business, and they all come a cropper, sooner or later.   I've seen hundreds of 'em.

CLARA (*with awe*).   Are you a real detective ?

CROWTHER.   Yes, I am.   Do I look like one ?

CLARA. You don't look like them on the pictures.

CROWTHER. Don't you take too much notice of the pictures. Give you wrong ideas. Life's not like the pictures.

CLARA (*wistfully*). No, I've noticed that. But I don't mind. I like the pictures.

(MISS TRACEY *enters* L.)

MISS TRACEY (*coming* O. *above the table*). Ah—Mr. Crowther—the detective——

CROWTHER (*rising slowly*). Yes, miss. (*To* CLARA.) Now off you go to bed, young woman.

CLARA (*going*). Good night. Good night, miss.

MISS TRACEY. Good night. (*She watches* CLARA *go, then turns to the table.*) Ah—sandwiches. What are they ?

CROWTHER. Ham.

MISS TRACEY. Excellent—I'm very fond of a ham sandwich——

(*She takes one.* CROWTHER *sits down.*)

That's right—sit down. Now, you're the very person I came down to find. I don't want to worry you while you're having your nice little supper and wanting to read your newspaper. By the way, we've met before, you know. (*She sits* O. *above the table.*)

CROWTHER. Yes, I thought we had. I don't often forget people. Part of my training, that.

MISS TRACEY (*briskly, between nibbles of her sandwich*). Isn't that splendid ? Yes, I remember the occasion. It was at the London hotel, and a friend of mine complained that she'd had her brooch stolen, and you said No, she must have lost it, and you were rather pig-headed about it, I remember. However, that's all over and done with, isn't it ? What I wanted to tell you is that I'm rather worried about my companion. You saw her, didn't you ?

CROWTHER (*rather ungraciously*). No, but I heard you had somebody with you.

MISS TRACEY. That's right. Well, she's been put in

the room next to mine—there's a communicating door,
you know—and I thought I'd see if she was all right.
So I knocked on the door—and then, after a time—
when she didn't answer, I thought she must have fallen
asleep—and so I tried the door quietly—but it was
locked. So then I went round to the other door, outside on the corridor, and did the same thing there—
knocked and then tried to get in. But I couldn't.
That was locked too. And she didn't answer.

CROWTHER (*with a grin*). Well, perhaps she didn't
want to answer.

MISS TRACEY. You mean she's probably had enough
of me to-day——

CROWTHER (*still grinning*). I didn't say so.

MISS TRACEY. No, you looked it. But still, I can't
help feeling rather worried.

CROWTHER (*with a touch of contempt*). There's nothing
to worry about there.

MISS TRACEY. Well, I'm glad you think so. After
all, you're a detective. Did I tell you, I'm awfully
interested in detectives ?

CROWTHER (*satirically*). Read these detective tales,
eh ?

MISS TRACEY. Yes, hundreds of them. *Most* fas-
cinating. Don't you ?

CROWTHER. No. To a professional, they're a lot o'
silly nonsense.

MISS TRACEY. Yes, I can see they might be. Still,
they're fun, I think.

CROWTHER (*heavily patronizing*). And if you'll take
my advice, you'll stop thinking about detective tales
and mysteries and nonsense, and stop worrying about
your friend, just because she doesn't want to talk to
you. No mystery about that. And when there's a
real mystery here——

MISS TRACEY. You'll settle it for me, eh ?

CROWTHER. I'll do that all right.

(*He picks up his newspaper, as if to dismiss her. At this
moment, three explosions, which might be loud pistol*

shots some distance away, are heard off and above.
CROWTHER *jumps up, startled.* MISS TRACEY *looks at him, and then looks at her watch.*)

MISS TRACEY (*coolly*).   And the time is exactly seven minutes past ten.

BLACK OUT.

ACT II

Same as before. Next morning.

At the rise of the CURTAIN, *the following are grouped, standing, in a curved line from the door* R. *to the middle of the back wall, in this order from* R. *to* L. *:* KEITH, HELEN *(sitting on lower chair),* MRS. HEATON, EDNA SANDARS *(seated on arm of the upstage chair),* ARNOLD JORDAN, FRED, SALLY *and* CLARA. CROWTHER, *looking at once important but flustered, is standing facing them on the left. There is a moment's pause, while they wait for him to speak, and he marshals his thoughts. He has a notebook in his hand.*

CROWTHER. Now I've got you here, because we're going to start all over again. It's morning now and if there *is* any sense amongst us, perhaps we'll find it. You can't say now you're too sleepy and you're too cold or you're too frightened to think. So we'll start right from the beginning. You probably know it already, but I might as well remind you that if the telephone line hadn't broken down and if we hadn't been completely snowed up this morning, we'd have had the police here long before this. But we're cut off from everybody, and until we can get through again, *I'm* the police. That's right, isn't it, Mr. Henley ?

KEITH. Yes, that's right. (*To the others.*) You all understand that ? For the time being, Mr. Crowther is acting for the police. He's also acting as usual for the company, and as we're all employees of the company, we must help him.

CROWTHER. Thanks, Mr. Henley. (*To them all.*) And I don't propose to stand any nonsense from anybody this morning. Now, you're all here, aren't you ?

KEITH. Yes, all *our* people are. But Miss Tracey isn't here yet?

EDNA. Yes, what about her? She started all this——

CROWTHER. All right. I'll talk to her very soon. There are one or two things that she said last night I don't understand yet——

EDNA. I'll bet there are.

CROWTHER. That'll do from you. But Miss Tracey is the only one who's completely clear, because when it happened she was down here—talking to me. So don't you worry about her. What you've all got to do this morning is to start telling the truth and answering my questions properly. (*He pauses.*) Now I'll just put the situation to you again—quietly—just giving you the facts—before we all think we're going barmy. (*He glances at his notebook.*) At about ten minutes to ten, last night, an elderly lady—whose name has been given to me as Mrs. Jernigan—was shown up to her room here. I didn't see her myself—I happened to be up in my room when she came—but several of you did. (*He points to* CLARA.) You took her out of the car and showed her up to the room, didn't you?

CLARA. Yes, Mr. Crowther.

SALLY. And I saw her, when I was in there (*pointing off* R.), and Clara came past with her.

CROWTHER. Right. (*He glances at his notebook.*) Four of you were in here when she came through. Mr. Henley, Mrs. Heaton, Mr. Jordan, Miss Sandars—that right?

(*The four in question nod agreement or say " Yes."*)

This Mrs. Jernigan is shown into her room. There's a communicating door between her room and Miss Tracey's. But Mrs. Jernigan locks this door and also locks the door into the corridor——

EDNA (*sharply*). How do you know she did?

CROWTHER. Because when Miss Tracey comes down here to see me—at ten o'clock or a minute or two past—she complains to me that both these doors are locked and that Mrs. Jernigan doesn't answer her when she knocks. That's why she came to see me, to tell me that. I didn't think anything of it—why should I ? I think this Mrs. Jernigan's had enough of Miss Tracey for one day and wants to go to sleep. At exactly seven minutes past ten, I hear three explosions—they might be shots and then again they might not—and I go upstairs, Miss Tracey following me, find some of you people out on the landing. Mr. Henley, whose room was the nearest to these rooms the ladies occupied, swears that the noise came from the far room—Mrs. Jernigan's. We can't get into that room. We break the lock of the door leading into the corridor, and then we find that Mrs. Jernigan has disappeared. We know that the door we had to break down was locked on the inside. The communicating door was locked on the inside. All the windows were fastened. (*To* KEITH.) There's no doubt about that, is there ?

KEITH. No. I'll swear to that. The windows were fastened, and the two doors had been locked on the inside.

CROWTHER. Yes, the keys were there, turned in the locks. With the room like that, nobody could have got in. And she couldn't have got out, dead or alive.

JORDAN (*eagerly*). But, Mr. Crowther, perhaps she never went into that room. That may be the explanation. Only Clara says she went in there——

CLARA (*indignantly*). Well, I ought to know, oughtn't I ? Didn't I take her in ? Think I'm lying, or what ?

CROWTHER. Well, that's not impossible, y'know. I'm willing to bet money that a lot of lies, deliberate lies, were told me last night, but I'm going to have the truth this morning.

CLARA (*desperately, almost crying*). I tell you I took her in——

CROWTHER. All right, all right. I know you did. (*To* JORDAN.) Don't you see, she must have done ? There was Mrs. Jernigan's bag, in the middle of the floor, lying open. Between the bed and the window there was a handkerchief—with some spots of blood on it——

SALLY. Oo, if I'd known that last night, I couldn't have slept a wink. Blood !

CROWTHER. There were also two bits of paper, very valuable pieces of evidence.

EDNA. You haven't told us yet what was written on those pieces of paper.

CROWTHER. No, and I'm not going to. And the last thing is, there's plenty of evidence that those three explosions—the shots or whatever they were—came from that room. You could smell the powder. You could see some of it. (*Angrily.*) Now does anybody want to tell me that an empty room unlocked Mrs. Jernigan's bag, put two pieces of paper on the floor, sprinkled blood on a handkerchief, and then fired three shots ? No. Mrs. Jernigan went into that room. And somebody else went into that room, too.

FRED. Listen, Mr. Crowther. Couldn't somebody have been in the room when she went in ? I mean, hiding in the wardrobe or behind the window curtains ?

CROWTHER. Yes, Fred, I've thought of that.

MRS. HEATON. There wasn't anybody in there five minutes before Mrs. Jernigan went in, because I drew the curtains myself while Sally and Clara made the bed.

FRED. Did you look in the wardrobe ?

MRS. HEATON. Yes, I looked specially, to see if the manager had left any things in there. I knew it was one of his two rooms.

HELEN. But, Mrs. Heaton, after you left—and before Clara came back with Mrs. Jernigan—the door into the corridor was open, wasn't it ?

MRS. HEATON. Yes. Someone could have got in then.

KEITH. But if someone got in—and someone must have done—how did they get out again ?

JORDAN. Mrs. Jernigan could have let them out——

CROWTHER (*sneering, loudly*). Yes, and then fired three shots and completely disappeared, eh ?

EDNA. One of the Maskelyne and Devant girls. At lunch-time she'll probably pop out of the coffee-pot.

HELEN (*cuttingly*). I don't think this business is very funny, y'know, Miss Sandars.

EDNA. Don't you ? I think it's a scream.

CROWTHER. Well, you're soon going to change your mind about that. I'll have no funny work from anybody this morning. (*He pauses.*) Well, those are the facts. We looked in every room in this hotel last night. We'll have to look again to-day. In the meantime, I'm going to start asking questions all over again. I'll take you one at a time in here, and until I want you, you can be getting on with whatever you have to do.

FRED. We can go now, then, eh, Mr. Crowther ?

CROWTHER. Until I send for you. And don't forget, everybody, I'm not standing for any more fairy-tales. Some of you are lying, and the sooner you start telling the truth the better. (*To* KEITH, *indicating the two maids*.) One of these two had better wait out there (*indicating the door* L.), to fetch the others when I want 'em.

MRS. HEATON (*to* KEITH). Take Clara. I want Sally to help me.

KEITH. All right, Clara. You wait outside. The rest of you can carry on.

(JORDAN *exits* R., *the remainder* L. KEITH *turns to* CROWTHER *after the others have gone*.)

You'd better begin with me.

CROWTHER. All right.

(KEITH *lights a cigarette*.)

Now then. (*Crossing* R. *to* KEITH.) You were in your room at seven minutes past ten last night, eh ?

KEITH. Yes. I'm sorry, Crowther, but I can't tell you anything different from what I told you last night. I was in my room, and was half-undressed when those reports went off. I was rather startled, of course, but I thought it was only somebody fooling. So I finished undressing, put my pyjamas on, then thought I'd better investigate, so put on a dressing-gown and went out——

CROWTHER. And I met you outside on the landing.

(*He is interrupted by the entrance, brisk and smiling, of* MISS TRACEY.)

MISS TRACEY. Good morning. Sorry I'm so late. (*To* CROWTHER.) Have you solved the mystery yet?

CROWTHER (*patiently, rather wearily*). No. I'm just getting down to it properly. I've had the whole lot of 'em in front of me, and now I'm taking them one by one.

MISS TRACEY (*eagerly*). Splendid! You must let me help you. I think I told you I'm awfully interested in this detective business. I read all the good detective stories (*sitting* c. *above the table*), and a lot of bad ones too.

CROWTHER. Yes, you did tell me, Miss Tracey. And the sooner you forget about those detective tales, the better. Don't expect me to find two specks of tobacco-ash, tell you which of fifty kinds it is, and then announce that the crime was committed by a left-handed red-haired man who used to live in Hong-Kong.

MISS TRACEY. All right, I won't. All I ask is that you let me help. I promise not to be a nuisance. And —you never know—I might spot something that you might miss.

CROWTHER. I don't think you will. But you can try.

MISS TRACEY. Thank you, Mr. Crowther. (*To* KEITH.) I'm sorry this has happened, of course, but I must say the whole thing seems to me the *greatest* fun. I wouldn't have missed it for anything.

CROWTHER (*who has been looking at his notebook, to* KEITH). Oh—there's one thing I wanted to ask you. Had you ever seen this Mrs. Jernigan before?

KEITH. I don't know. You see—I never saw her face properly.

MISS TRACEY. Isn't it odd? Neither did I.

CROWTHER (*astounded*). *What!*

MISS TRACEY. No, I never saw her face properly either.

CROWTHER. But she was your companion, wasn't she?

MISS TRACEY. She was my companion in the car on the way up here, certainly. My fellow traveller, not my *paid* companion, not that sort of companion. Good gracious, you don't think I'm the kind of woman who'd have some tame pussy-cat of a female to read to her and fill hot-water bottles ?

CROWTHER. Mrs. Jernigan was a friend, then ?

MISS TRACEY (*heartily*). Certainly not. Didn't know the woman at all.

CROWTHER (*bewildered*). But I was just going to ask you about her.

MISS TRACEY. No use asking *me* about her. Couldn't tell you anything except that she said her name was Mrs. Jernigan.

CROWTHER. But what was she doing in your car ?

MISS TRACEY. I gave her a lift here. You see, when I left the hotel at Market Harborough, this woman was standing at the door and said her car had broken down. She wanted to come on here, so I said I'd bring her here.

CROWTHER. Now wait a minute. Let me get this straight. She didn't come here because you were coming here ?

MISS TRACEY. No, the opposite. I came because *she* wanted to come.

CROWTHER (*suspiciously*). You didn't say so, last night.

MISS TRACEY. Nobody asked me, last night.

CROWTHER. Then she's a stranger to you ?

MISS TRACEY. Complete stranger. Not sorry either. She seemed a very dull woman, though I may have misjudged her, for there's nothing dull about the way she's gone on here, is there ?

CROWTHER. Well, this makes it crazier than ever. We don't know *anything* about the woman. I'll have to go through that suitcase of hers very carefully.

KEITH. That's your only chance.

MISS TRACEY (*coolly and cheerfully*). I'm afraid that's no use either.

CROWTHER. Why ?

MISS TRACEY. Because, you see, that's not her suit-case, it's mine.

CROWTHER (*angry and bewildered*). Well—for the love of Mike !——

MISS TRACEY. You see, she came away in such a hurry with me, she forgot to take her own luggage out of her car, so I re-arranged my things and let her have that suitcase. Not everything, y'know. No extra toothbrush, for instance.

CROWTHER (*testily*). Oh—never mind toothbrushes! (*Crossing* L. *at back.*) Ah—but wait a minute! (*He produces an envelope, and brings out two scraps of paper.*) Did these come out of your bag? (*At* L. *of* MISS TRACEY.)

MISS TRACEY. I don't recognize them. What are they?

CROWTHER. One's a name and address. You're not going to see that just now. The other's a fragment of a letter.

(*He hands it over.* KEITH *looks at it over* MISS TRACEY'S *right shoulder.*)

MISS TRACEY (*reading slowly*). "If you try to interfere you will "—" and it will not be the first time "—" mind yours and we will mind ours "—" ing for trouble." I suppose that's "looking for trouble."

CROWTHER. Yes, sure to be.

MISS TRACEY (*handing it back*). Splendid! It reads like a warning letter from a gang. Is it?

CROWTHER. I shouldn't be surprised.

MISS TRACEY. Some people have all the luck.

CROWTHER. Call that luck, do you? I'll bet she isn't calling it luck, wherever she is.

MISS TRACEY. Yes, but where is she?

CROWTHER. Probably somewhere in this hotel—out.

MISS TRACEY. Dead?

CROWTHER. Dead as mutton, if you ask me. And the body hidden away somewhere.

MISS TRACEY. But how did they get it out of the room then, with the two doors locked inside and all the windows fastened?

CROWTHER (*testily*). I don't know. (*Down* L.) There's a catch in it somewhere, of course. And whoever did it was either one of the staff here or was working with one of the staff. A complete stranger couldn't have managed it.

KEITH. Are you certain ?

CROWTHER. Yes, how would he know which room she was going in ?

(KEITH *works down* R.)

MISS TRACEY. How would he know she was coming here at all ?

CROWTHER. Because she may have told somebody she was coming here.

KEITH. But *why* was she coming here ?

CROWTHER (*triumphantly, crossing* R. *to* KEITH *in front of the table*). Ah—now that's something I think I *do* know.

KEITH (*incredulously*). No !

CROWTHER (*with irritating air of mystification*). Yes. That's the one thing about the whole business that's fairly clear to me.

MISS TRACEY. And now you'll tell us, eh ?

CROWTHER (*putting two papers back*). No, I shan't. I'll keep that bit to myself.

MISS TRACEY (*severely*). I hope you're not going to be one of those irritating detectives who never say anything until they've called everybody together in the library in the last chapter. Don't just put us off with, " Notice the position of the cruet."

CROWTHER (*who has not been listening*). What cruet ?

MISS TRACEY. All right. There isn't a cruet.

CROWTHER (*looks at his notebook and then at* KEITH). I think I've got these rooms right. Next to yours is an empty bedroom, then there's Mrs. Heaton, then Miss Tennant, then another empty room, then mine, and Jordan's next to me. Eh ?

KEITH. Yes. The other four are on the floor above. Fred's just to the left at the top of the stairs. Edna Sandars is the first along the landing to the right, and the two maids are sharing a room further along.

CROWTHER. Yes, I've got that. Well, I'll take 'em in that order then. So Mrs. Heaton'll be next.

KEITH (*crossing* L. *and calling*).   Clara.

(CLARA *pops her head in.*)

Ask Mrs. Heaton to come down.

(CLARA *disappears.*)

You don't want me, do you ?

CROWTHER.   No.   Oh—there's just one other thing. While you were in your room, did you hear anything or did anything happen that was the least bit out of the ordinary ?

KEITH.   No, I don't think so.   Oh !—(*Working down* L. *and then to* L.C.)   The only thing was this.   After I'd been up there a minute or two, somebody knocked softly on the door.   I called out, " Yes, what is it ? " Nothing happened.   So I looked out, and I saw Arnold Jordan walking away——

CROWTHER (*eagerly*).   Which way ?

KEITH.   Not towards Mrs. Jernigan's room, but the other way.

CROWTHER (*disappointed*).   Is that all ?

KEITH.   Well—no, not quite.   While I was looking, Mrs. Heaton, who's next to me, looked out too, and then, when she saw me, she shut the door again.   That's all.

CROWTHER.   It's something.   Here's one of 'em prowling about, knocking at doors and then walking away, and here's another of 'em looking out into the corridor in a suspicious manner.   It'll have to be accounted for. I'll get the truth out of 'em this morning, you'll see.

MISS TRACEY (*with enthusiasm*).   And you must let me help.   I've always wanted an excuse to ask a lot of people the most impudent and intimate questions.

CROWTHER.   I don't know about that, Miss Tracey. You take it easy.

(MRS. HEATON *enters* L., *very quiet and composed.   She comes to* L. *of the table.*)

KEITH.   I'm going along to my office—if you want me again.

(*He goes out* L.)

CROWTHER (*at* R. *of the table*).   Now then, Mrs. Heaton.

MRS. HEATON.   I'm afraid I told you all I know last night, Mr. Crowther.

CROWTHER (*in rather hectoring tone*).   We'll see about that.

MISS TRACEY (*smiling at her*).   Good morning, Mrs. Heaton.   (*She is still seated.*)

MRS. HEATON.   Good morning, Miss Tracey.   (*To* CROWTHER.)   Yes ?

CROWTHER.   Where's Mr. Heaton ?

MRS. HEATON (*startled*).   What ?

CROWTHER.   You're Mrs. Heaton, aren't you ?   Well, then, where's Mr. Heaton ?   (*As she hesitates, confused and indignant.*)   Now don't tell me it's no business of mine.   People have been saying that to me for the last twenty years.   They forget that when a serious crime is being investigated, everything about the people who might be concerned in it is important.

MISS TRACEY (*gently, encouragingly*).   I think that's true, Mrs. Heaton.   Though of course you needn't answer questions if you don't want to.

CROWTHER (*rather angrily*).   I say, who's conducting this investigation ?

MISS TRACEY.   Both of us.

MRS. HEATON.   Well—if you must know—there isn't a Mr. Heaton.   Heaton is my own name.

CROWTHER.   Then you're really Miss Heaton ?

MRS. HEATON (*hesitantly*).   Yes.

CROWTHER.   Then why do you wear a wedding ring ?

MISS TRACEY (*as* MRS. HEATON *hesitates*).   I think it would be better if you admitted you were married.

MRS. HEATON.   All right, I *am* married, but when I'm working for the company, I don't use my married name.

CROWTHER.   Why ?

MRS. HEATON.   I'm sorry, but it's got nothing to do with—this business—so I shan't tell you.

CROWTHER.   All right, you won't, then.   But you admit you're married and—for reasons best known to yourself—you don't use your husband's name.   (*He*

looks at his notebook.)   You specially asked to be trans-
ferred up here this season, didn't you ?   Why ?

MRS. HEATON.   Why shouldn't I ?

CROWTHER.   I'm not asking you why you shouldn't,
I'm asking you why you did.

MRS. HEATON.   Well—for the same reason that a lot
of hotel people ask for transfers—I wanted a change.

CROWTHER.   That's all you're going to say about
it, eh ?

MRS. HEATON.   Yes.   I'm sorry, but I really haven't
any more to say that would be of the least interest to
you.

CROWTHER.   Oh, yes—you have.   There's something
you've never mentioned yet.   Last night, about ten
o'clock, just the time that's important, you suddenly
looked out of your room, and then when you saw Mr.
Henley looking out of *his* room, you withdrew again in
a hurry.   Why ?

MRS. HEATON (*puzzled*).   Mr. Henley himself must
have told you that.

MISS TRACEY.   Yes, he did.

CROWTHER (*annoyed, to* MISS TRACEY).   Who's doing
this ?   What do you want to go and tell her that for ?

MISS TRACEY.   Because she's a sensible woman—and
I believe an honest one—and we ought to deal sensibly
and honestly with her.

MRS. HEATON.   Thank you, Miss Tracey.   (*To both
of them.*)   It was chiefly because of Mr. Henley that I
didn't say anything about it before.   You see, my bedroom is next but one to Mr. Henley's—the one between
isn't being used—and on the other side, with only a
very thin wall between us, is Miss Tennant.   I heard
Miss Tennant moving about in her room, and then I
thought I heard somebody else there—it sounded like
a man.

MISS TRACEY.   Dear, dear, dear !

CROWTHER (*triumphantly*).   You see what happens
when you start getting the truth out of 'em.   It's
always the same.   (*To* MRS. HEATON.)   Well ?

MRS. HEATON.   I was—rather worried—about this.

Then I thought I must have been mistaken. But just
then somebody seemed to go past my door. So I looked
out. Then I saw Mr. Henley looking out, and I felt
rather embarrassed and didn't want him to think I was
spying on him, so I got back again.

Miss Tracey. You like Mr. Henley?

Mrs. Heaton. Well, I only met him for the first time
two days ago—we've both been with the company for
some years, but never working in the same hotel—so I
don't know much about him, but he seems a very
pleasant young man.

Crowther. What did you think when you saw him
looking out? (*As she hesitates.*) Come on, you might
as well say it. You thought he'd just got back to his
own room from Miss Tennant's, didn't you?

Mrs. Heaton (*hesitantly*). Yes, I did.

Miss Tracey. Why? Just because he was looking
out? Why should he look out if he's just been out?

Crowther. To see if anybody had noticed him.

Miss Tracey. It sounds silly to me. If I'd been out
of my room and didn't want anybody to see me, I'd
get back as quickly as I could, without peeping about.

Mrs. Heaton (*hesitantly*). Yes, I thought of that.
But you see, Miss Tennant's a very attractive girl—and
I'd noticed that Mr. Henley was being very attentive
to her—and I thought he must have made some excuse
to see her for a moment in her room. It was nothing
to do with me, of course——

Crowther (*quickly, forcefully*). It's something to do
with me, though, if he's been lying. I'm going to have
another look at those rooms.

(*He goes out L. Miss Tracey and Mrs. Heaton look at
each other.*)

Mrs. Heaton (*troubled*). I didn't want to say anything. I'm not at all an interfering, spying sort of
person, and I'm sure I must seem one——

Miss Tracey (*heartily*). No, you don't. Not to me,
anyhow. I said last night—and I still think so this
morning—that you seemed a very nice woman. I also

said you seemed rather unhappy. I know you are now,
and I think I know why.

MRS. HEATON (*very quietly, troubled*). Yes, I'm not
very happy just now. (*She moves away* L.)

MISS TRACEY. All right, we won't talk about it.
But you might tell me why you wanted to be trans-
ferred up here. You don't look the sort of woman who
likes changing about for its own sake. Where were you
before ?

MRS. HEATON. At the Bournemouth hotel.

MISS TRACEY. I thought you were. And now you
must tell me, and I'm not asking out of idle curiosity.
What made you want to leave the Bournemouth hotel ?
(*As she hesitates to reply, looking sharply at her.*) Was
some man on the staff there making a nuisance of
himself ?

MRS. HEATON. Yes.

MISS TRACEY (*grimly*). Which of them was it ?

MRS. HEATON (*agitated*). No, it wasn't like that at all.
(*Crossing* R.) I can't tell you who it was, that wouldn't
be fair. But it wasn't his fault. It was mine.

MISS TRACEY. You mean—that he was serious about
you—and you couldn't explain to him about your
marriage ?

MRS. HEATON. Yes. It was—too difficult—to explain—and I was rather ashamed too—so I felt the only
thing was to leave. So I asked to be sent up here.

MISS TRACEY (*rather sharply*). But now you aren't
any happier, are you ? Things are more difficult, instead of being easier ?

MRS. HEATON. How do you know ?

MISS TRACEY. My dear, I'm an elderly woman and
no fool, and I've nobody to bother about except one or
two healthy nephews and nieces. I've no drama going
on inside, as all you people have. So I can give all
my time and energy to noticing what other people are
like. You've no idea what a lot you do notice once
you've stopped leading an intense personal life yourself.
It's people like me who ought to be the detectives.
That's why I'm enjoying all this.

MRS. HEATON. Enjoying it! And that poor woman
—— !

MISS TRACEY (*briskly*). I shouldn't bother my head
too much about that poor woman, if I were you.

(MRS. HEATON *stares at her in shocked surprise.* EDNA
enters R., *carrying a cup of coffee.*)

EDNA. Ah!—the great detective *has* gone upstairs?

MRS. HEATON. Yes, but what are *you* doing down
here, Miss Sandars?

EDNA. Having my morning coffee.

MRS. HEATON (*rather unpleasantly*). So I see. Well, *I*
must go back to my work.

(*She goes out* L. EDNA *perches herself on the lower* R.
corner of the table.)

EDNA. Good morning, Miss Tracey. Enjoying yourself?

MISS TRACEY. Yes.

EDNA (*coolly*). I thought you were. (*She pauses.*)
Like some coffee?

MISS TRACEY. No, thank you.

EDNA. Perhaps you're right. It's rather foul.

MISS TRACEY (*rising and crossing down* R.). Mrs.
Heaton doesn't seem to approve of you.

EDNA. No, she doesn't. I don't approve of her
much.

MISS TRACEY. Why? She seems to me a very nice
woman.

EDNA. I know. I don't like nice women much.
Too soft. I'm one of the tough ones.

MISS TRACEY (*politely, with a shade of irony*). That
must be fun for you. Is this your first season up here?

EDNA. Yes. I blew in with this jolly little advance
guard two days ago.

MISS TRACEY. And how are you getting on?

EDNA. Well, so far I'm about as popular as a stiff
dose of influenza.

MISS TRACEY. But you don't mind—being tough?

EDNA. No. I'm used to it. (*She pauses.*) Tell *me*

something now, Miss Tracey. Why did *you* come here ?

MISS TRACEY. I've just explained to Mr. Crowther that I happened to come here because the poor woman who's disappeared, Mrs. Jernigan, wanted to come here, and I had offered to give her a lift.

EDNA (*putting her coffee-cup on the table*). That's what you explained to Crowther ?

MISS TRACEY. Yes.

EDNA. Quite. Now tell *me* why you came here.

MISS TRACEY (*rather enjoying herself*). Young woman, you're not accusing me of giving an entirely false account of my actions, are you ?

EDNA. Yes, of course I am.

MISS TRACEY. Well, really——

EDNA. All right. Please yourself. (*She pauses, then smiles.*) I hear you're very fond of detective stories.

MISS TRACEY. Yes, I am.

EDNA (*with enigmatic smile*). So am I. And I often have quite a lot of time for reading on my job.

(*Enter* CROWTHER L., *looking triumphant. He comes down* L.)

CROWTHER. I've found something—— (*He notices* EDNA.) Hello !

EDNA (*with burlesque social manner*). Hello ! What extraordinary weather we're having, aren't we ?

CROWTHER. When I want you down here, Miss Sandars, I'll send for you.

EDNA (*airily*). Any time you feel that the case is too much for you, Inspector——

CROWTHER. Outside.

(EDNA *moves slowly towards the door* R. CROWTHER *moves* L.C. *to* MISS TRACEY.)

Yes, I've found something. Up in Keith Henley's room——

EDNA (*whirling round, near the door*). Now, just a minute, Mr. Crowther. I don't know what you've found——

CROWTHER. No, and you're not going to know.

EDNA. But if you take anything found in anybody's room now as evidence, you must be crazy. Don't you realize that for the last two hours anything could have been planted in anybody's room ? (*She pauses.*) Except mine. (*She holds up a key.*) It's locked, and there's the key. (*She holds up a second key.*) And there's the other key. And there aren't any more.

CROWTHER (*raising his voice*). I want one of those keys. (*He crosses* R.)

EDNA. You're probably not the only one.

(*She goes out* R., *banging the door in his face.*)

CROWTHER. I'll deal with her later on. She's got a lot of trouble coming to her, whether she's in this or not.

MISS TRACEY (*coming down* R.). What did you find in Mr. Henley's room ?

CROWTHER (*grinning*). I found a certain name and address. (*He produces a card from his pocket, but does not let her read it.*) And believe it or not, that name and address provide a definite link with Mrs. Jernigan.

MISS TRACEY. You mean, there was the same name and the same address on the other bit of paper you found in her room ?

CROWTHER. Now that's smart of you, Miss Tracey, very smart. How did you guess ?

MISS TRACEY. You wouldn't tell me what was on that other bit of paper. You say this name and address provide a link. What other link could there be ?

CROWTHER. Well, we'll find out what Mr. Keith Henley really did last night before we're much older. I've got the girl coming in next—Miss Tennant. Not that I think she's been mixed up in this business. Not the type, I should say.

MISS TRACEY. You may be right. But it was quite possible for somebody to have put that card you found in Mr. Henley's room this morning, wasn't it ? (*She sits as before.*)

CROWTHER. Possible, but not likely. And anyhow, he's lying.

(*Enter* HELEN L., *composed and charming.*)

HELEN (*crossing* R. *behind* MISS TRACEY). You wanted to see me, I think, Mr. Crowther.

CROWTHER. Yes, Miss Tennant. One or two more questions I want to ask.

HELEN (*smiling*). Certainly. (*To* MISS TRACEY.) Good morning.

MISS TRACEY. Good morning. Great fun this, isn't it?

HELEN (*earnestly*). No, I don't think it *is* fun, if you don't mind my saying so. It's all too horrible. That poor woman—probably lying dead somewhere in the hotel—it's absolutely horrible. Surely you must feel that?

MISS TRACEY. No, can't say I do. It's time some of us useless old things began disappearing. We take up too much of other people's time.

CROWTHER. Now then, Miss Tracey. None of that sort of talk or else I'll begin to suspect *you*. Besides, you don't know that Mrs. Jernigan *was* a useless old thing. I'm beginning to think she wasn't. Miss Tennant, you told me you went straight upstairs to your room last night, spoke to nobody, saw nobody, until those three bangs brought everybody out.

HELEN. Yes, that's true.

CROWTHER. But now I understand that Keith Henley came to your room, about ten o'clock, and talked to you for a minute or two.

HELEN (*indignantly*). Certainly not. I never saw or spoke to Mr. Henley after I left him just outside this door, when I went up to bed. Until, of course, we all came out.

CROWTHER. He didn't come to your room?

HELEN. No. Why should he? Who said he did?

CROWTHER. Nobody came to your room, then?

HELEN. No.

MISS TRACEY. Are you sure, Miss Tennant?

HELEN. Yes—no, I'm sorry. I'm forgetting——

CROWTHER. Ah—you're forgetting. Now then, let's have it, please.

HELEN. Well, it was so unimportant, it was easy to

forget. There was a knock at my door. I went to see who it was. It was Mr. Jordan. He said, "Oh, I'm sorry. I'm looking for Keith Henley." That's exactly what happened.

CROWTHER (*in some excitement*). Now wait a minute! What are we going to make out of this? That's practically the same story Keith Henley told. There was a knock at *his* door, and when he looked out, he saw Jordan walking away. And you say Jordan knocked at *your* door and said he was looking for Henley. Now what's Jordan doing, knocking at doors and walking away? It doesn't make sense.

HELEN. Well, that's exactly what happened. (*She crosses down* R.)

CROWTHER. Mrs. Heaton, who's next door to you, says she heard somebody enter your room and then heard your voices.

HELEN (*calmly*). She's mistaken. She must have heard me answering the door when Mr. Jordan knocked. After all, why *should* anybody come to my room at that time?

CROWTHER (*excitedly*). It's no use asking me that. I could ask dozens. Why should everybody start wandering about and knocking at doors? Why should everybody tell lies or forget what happened to them? Why should an elderly lady disappear out of a locked room? I could go on for an hour.

MISS TRACEY. It might be a good idea if you did, y'know, only I think you ought to do it by yourself.

HELEN. I'm afraid I've nothing else to tell you.

CROWTHER. That's the favourite remark here. And then it turns out you *have* something else.

(*Enter* SALLY L., *excitedly*.)

SALLY (*almost breathless*). Here, I say, Mr. Crowther, what right has that Edna Sandars to go snooping round that room where it happened?

CROWTHER (*hastily*). Is she in there now?

SALLY. Yes, poking about and picking things up——

CROWTHER (*crossing* L. *up stage*).   I'll have her out of that, the saucy 'ussy !

(*He hurries out, followed by* SALLY.   MISS TRACEY *and* HELEN *look at each other and smile.*)

MISS TRACEY.   How did you come into this hotel life, Miss Tennant ?

HELEN (*up to top* R. *corner of the table*).   Well, the money began to run out, you know—as it so often does with people nowadays—and I was good at games and could get on with people—so I started with one or two little winter sports jobs as hostess in Switzerland—and then, last year, this company took me on and sent me down to their hotel at Cannes.

MISS TRACEY.   Let me see, wasn't Mrs. Morrison acting as hostess and games organizer there ?

HELEN.   Yes, I went as her assistant.

MISS TRACEY.   Did you like Mrs. Morrison ?

HELEN (*with sweet enthusiasm*).   Oh—yes—I thought she was a darling.   She was sweet to me and we had a lovely time.

MISS TRACEY.   Wasn't that nice ?   But you preferred to come here ?

HELEN.   Well, I was sorry to leave Cannes, of course, but I was only the assistant there, and here I was offered the whole thing.   I'm terribly keen on being a success here, of course.   That's why I thought I'd look in so early to see how things were.   I do hope this awful business, when it gets into the papers, won't spoil our season.

MISS TRACEY (*dryly*).   Awful businesses never keep people away, my dear.   They attract 'em.   But I have a feeling we may be able to keep all this out of the papers.   Being snowed up is probably a bit of luck for us.

(*Enter* JORDAN *from* R.   *He looks rather excited.*)

JORDAN.   Where is Mr. Crowther ?

HELEN (*moving away* R.).   He went upstairs, Mr. Jordan.

Miss Tracey. Ah—yes—now you're Mr. Jordan, of course.

Jordan (*excitedly*). Yes, and you are Miss Tracey (*up to her*), the visitor who arrived much too early and brought us all this trouble. And now we recognize one another. Good morning. How d'you do ?

Miss Tracey (*coolly*). I'm having a most delightful time, thank you.

Jordan (*with luxuriant pessimism*). And I am having a hell of a time. I hate the kitchen. I hate the hotel. We are all snowed in. An old lady has probably been murdered. Nobody knows how it has been done. Nobody ever will know. We have the stupidest detective in Europe. Any old lady who allows herself to be murdered when he is about deserves to be murdered.

Miss Tracey (*delighted with him*). Now you be careful, Mr. Jordan.

Jordan. Why ? Why should I be careful ?

Miss Tracey. Because very soon Mr. Crowther will want to know why you go round knocking at doors at night. By the way, *did* you knock at Miss Tennant's door ?

Jordan. I don't remember, but if she says I did, then I did. (*He sits up stage* R.)

(*Enter* Crowther, *looking flustered, followed by* Edna.)

Crowther (*to* Edna). Now you sit there (*pointing*) and keep quiet.

(Edna *sits down* L. *with mock meekness.*)

(*To* Miss Tracey.) I don't want her in here, but I've either got to keep her under my eye or lock her up.

Miss Tracey. Then she must stay here. We can't begin locking people up. By the way, Mr. Jordan confirms Miss Tennant's story. He did knock at her door.

Crowther (*moving up to sideboard* c.). I see. (*To* Helen.) There's nothing else you forgot to tell me before, is there, Miss Tennant ?

Helen (*smiling*). No, there really isn't, this time.

Crowther. Well then—(*waving his hand, graciously*

for him) we needn't trouble you any longer. Thank you.

(HELEN *crosses to the door* L.)

EDNA (*in mock melodramatic tone*).   And thank you for bringing your pretty sweet face to light up our poor old home.

HELEN (*coming down to above* EDNA, *quite calmly*). I'm quite strong, y'know. And very soon, if you're not careful, I shall smack your face—hard.

CROWTHER (*with enthusiasm*).   Now you're talking, Miss Tennant !

HELEN (*continuing in a pleasant, even tone*).   You see, so far you've taken advantage of the fact that I'm new here and don't like rows. But I warn you that I've stood as much from you as I can stand.

(*She turns away, smiles at the others, then goes out* L.)

MISS TRACEY.   Plenty of spirit, that girl.

CROWTHER (*chuckling*).   A bit too much for our cheeky young friend here. Hasn't a word to say for herself now.

EDNA (*unabashed*).   Don't you believe it.

CROWTHER (*crossing down* L. *to* EDNA).   Here, you can write shorthand, can't you ? Have you got your note-book and pencil ?

EDNA.   Yes. And you'd be surprised if you knew what I'd written in my notebook with my pencil.

CROWTHER.   I'm not interested. But you can just make yourself useful while you are here by taking a note of what people say.

EDNA (*bringing out the notebook*).   It will be a pleasure, Mr. Holmes.

CROWTHER (*belligerently, crossing to* JORDAN).   Now then, Jordan, I think it's time we were hearing something from you, isn't it ?

JORDAN (*coming forward*).   All right. But I have nothing to tell you——

(*Both are* R.C.)

CROWTHER (*broadly*).   D'you hear that ? Another of

'em. Nothing to tell us. And everybody who's told their tale down here this morning has brought you into it.

JORDAN (*staggered*). What?

CROWTHER. Yes. Knocking at doors. So far as I can see, as soon as you got upstairs last night, you began knocking at doors. Now what's the idea?

JORDAN (*calmly*). There is no idea.

CROWTHER (*astounded*). What?

JORDAN (*louder, but calm*). I say there *is* no idea. I knock at doors. Very well, I knock at doors.

EDNA. Do I take this down, Dr. Thorndyke?

CROWTHER (*reproachfully to* JORDAN). Now this isn't getting us anywhere.

MISS TRACEY. We'd love to know *why* you knock at so many doors, Mr. Jordan.

JORDAN (*rather desperately now*). I have told you. I am the sort of man who knocks at doors. That does not mean I am a criminal. I do not kidnap or murder old ladies.

EDNA. He just knocks at doors. It's an old French custom.

CROWTHER. Now listen. You knock at one door and say you're looking for Keith Henley. You knock at Keith Henley's door and then just walk away. At least, that's what *he* says. Now how do you account for that?

JORDAN (*shrugging*). I do not account for it.

CROWTHER (*shouting*). Then you'd better start accounting for it. Mrs. Jernigan came to this hotel last night. Somebody fired three shots in her room. There's blood on her handkerchief. And she's missing.

JORDAN (*shouting back*). But I did not fire shots in her room or spill blood on her handkerchief or throw her body out of the window. I am only the man who knocks at doors.

CROWTHER. Yes, but why—why? You're talking as if you were barmy.

JORDAN. I think I *am* barmy.

CROWTHER. Yes, and we'll all be barmy soon.

EDNA (*after a pause*). May I put in a word, Inspector French?

CROWTHER (*disgustedly*). No.

MISS TRACEY. Yes. Go on.

EDNA. I use ze little grey cells. I see it all now. This isn't Arnold Jordan. He disappeared last night. This is Mrs. Jernigan, disguised as Arnold Jordan and she knocks at doors because she's trying to find her room.

CROWTHER (*furious*). Will you get out of here ?

EDNA (*hurriedly rising and moving up* L.). Yes, of course. Just what I want——

CROWTHER (*stopping her*). No, stay where you are, I was forgetting.

(EDNA *returns to her seat.* CROWTHER *turns to* JORDAN.)

All right. If you won't talk, you won't. But don't imagine you're going to get away with it.

JORDAN. I have nothing more to tell you. And I have nothing to get away with. You are making a foolish mistake, my friend.

(*He goes out* R. CROWTHER *wipes his forehead, groaning.*)

CROWTHER. You see, every one of 'em has something to hide. The whole case is crazy to start with, and now they're all making it crazier still.

MISS TRACEY (*brightly*). I suppose we couldn't start looking at fingerprints. I've always wanted to do that.

CROWTHER. You talk as if we were playing a parlour game. There's a catch in this somewhere——

EDNA. I wouldn't be surprised.

CROWTHER. I'm going to have another look at that room before I ask any more questions. (*Fiercely, to* EDNA.) You stay here. No more prowling round for you.

EDNA (*with mock meekness*). Yes, sir.

(CROWTHER *goes out* L. MISS TRACEY *and* EDNA *look at each other.*)

MISS TRACEY. I don't know what Mr. Jordan's playing at. But I'm sure he's as innocent as a baby.

EDNA (*calmly*). Of course he is. Anybody but Crowther could tell that just by looking at him.

MISS TRACEY. But I'd like to know why he went round last night knocking at doors.

EDNA (*calmly, crossing to lower* L. *corner of the table and lighting a cigarette*). I'll tell you if you'll promise not to repeat it to Crowther, who'll only spoil it all.

MISS TRACEY (*eagerly*). Of course I'll promise.

EDNA. Jordan was looking for his wife's room.

MISS TRACEY. His wife ? No, don't tell me. I can guess. (*She pauses a second, then comes to* L. *of* EDNA.) He's Mrs. Heaton's husband.

EDNA. Of course he is.

MISS TRACEY. Yes, I see now. How did *you* know ?

EDNA. I guessed it last night. He was saying to us that he ought to broadcast, and she said, " Who'd listen to *you*." Now she's a nice, rather soft, very conventional and polite creature, and the *only* man she'd say that to would be her husband, especially if she'd had a row with him.

MISS TRACEY. I said last night, at once, you were a sharp young woman.

EDNA. It also explains why he asked to come here. He was chief assistant chef at our London hotel, and he's the kind of man who'd rather be in London than up here. But when he heard that she was coming here, he asked to come too. I thought from the first there was something queer about them. Obviously what happened was that they married secretly, then they had a row soon afterwards, probably bust up for the time, and now of course they have to keep it quiet until they can make it up again.

MISS TRACEY. He must want to make it up—or he wouldn't have come here——

EDNA. No, and he wouldn't be trying to find her room. She's being the grand proud one. These soft women are often terribly obstinate once they've been really hurt.

MISS TRACEY. We ought to do something about them.

EDNA. That's easily worked. She's obviously still in love with him—or she wouldn't be so miserable—and we've only got to pile it on a bit about him being under suspicion—humph ?

MISS TRACEY.   I might have a word with her.

(*Enter* CLARA R., *looking alarmed.*)

Oh—do you know where Mrs. Heaton is ?

CLARA (*staying just inside the door*).   I think she's up in her room, ma'am.

(MISS TRACEY *goes out* L.   CLARA *looks at* EDNA *with round eyes.*)

EDNA (*crossing to her* R.C.).   Well, Clara, you're not looking too bright.

CLARA (*solemnly*).   Oo—Miss Sandars, I'm not feeling too bright. (*She drops her voice.*) I'm frightened.

EDNA.   You're not going to tell me you did it all.

CLARA (*passionately*).   Oo—Miss Sandars, I'd nothing to do with it.   Shots and blood-stained handkerchiefs ! It frightens me to think of 'em.   I've often read about things in the paper, but I never thought I'd be mixed up with 'em.   And if my mother knew, she wouldn't let me stay here another minute.

EDNA.   Well, your mother doesn't know and you can't get away.

CLARA.   Oo—I know.   And that makes it a lot worse. (*Coming closer, very confidentially.*) Miss Sandars, do they know who done it ?

EDNA (*with slight burlesque of same manner*).   No, Clara.   But Mr. Crowther thinks Mr. Jordan behaved in a very suspicious manner last night.

CLARA.   You don't think Mr. Jordan did it, do you ?

EDNA.   I don't know.

CLARA.   Do you think he might have dragged Sally into it ?

EDNA (*sharply, serious now*).   Sally ?   Why should he ? (*As* CLARA *hesitates.*) Come on.

CLARA (*very confidentially*).   Well, you see, Sally was going on a bit about Mr. Jordan just before we went to bed last night—what a nice man he was and all that— though I'd thought before that Fred was the chap she was after—and then when we got up to our bedroom, she went out and didn't say where she was going—and I don't know where she went—see ?

EDNA.   You haven't told anybody, have you ?

CLARA (*with increasing distress*).   Oo, no.   And don't you tell anybody I told you, Miss Sandars.   But, you see, Sally's been behaving queer ever since.   And I'm so frightened, Miss Sandars.   I can feel my heart going all the time.   I couldn't sleep last night at all, and every time I go into a room or open a cupboard (*crossing to the chair* c. *below the table*), I'm nearly sick—I think there'll be a body there—— (*She sits down and begins to cry.*)

EDNA.   Well, you needn't worry, there won't be.

CLARA (*sobbing*).   It's all right for you—but it was me that took that poor old lady up to that room—and——

EDNA (*decisively*).   I tell you it's all right.   You won't find Mrs. Jernigan's body in any room or cupboard.

CLARA (*still sobbing a little*).   You don't know.

EDNA.   I do.   I know for a fact that Mrs. Jernigan's body isn't in this hotel at all.

CLARA (*staring*).   But how do you know that ?

EDNA.   Never mind.   I *do* know.   So stop worrying about it.   You've absolutely nothing to worry about.

(*As* CLARA *is still staring at her and also dabbing her eyes,* CROWTHER *enters, followed by* FRED *and* SALLY. CROWTHER *moves to* L. *of the table,* SALLY *to above* L. *corner,* FRED *down* L.)

CROWTHER (*sharply*).   What's all this about ?

EDNA.   Nothing.   This kid was getting frightened, and I told her she'd nothing to worry about.

CROWTHER (*pugnaciously*).   Oh—*you* told her she'd nothing to worry about.

EDNA (*with equal pugnacity*).   Yes, *I* told her.   And don't you go frightening her all over again.

CROWTHER.   Ten to one she's hiding something or she wouldn't be so frightened.

CLARA (*in instant alarm*).   Oo—I'm not, I'm not really.

EDNA.   No, of course she isn't.   Leave her alone. See what you can make out of these two, instead.

FRED (*heartily*). That's all right to me. I can't tell you any more, Mr. Crowther. I went up to my room early last night. I stayed there until I heard all the commotion, and then I came out to see what was the matter. These two ladies hadn't even arrived when I went up to bed. I never set eyes on 'em, didn't know they were here.

CROWTHER (*agreeably*). No, that's true, Fred. I think we can leave you out of this. You went up to your room, stayed there, never spoke to anybody else until they all came out, eh?

FRED (*heartily*). That's right, Mr. Crowther. I'm ready to swear to that.

SALLY (*involuntarily*). Oh—Fred!——

FRED (*turning on her*). What do you mean, " Oh, Fred ! " ?

CROWTHER. Yes, let's hear something from you now, Sally What's-your-name. Now, as you know very well, it isn't the first time I've had to have a serious little talk with you——

SALLY (*disgustedly*). Aren't you ever going to forget that ?

CROWTHER. No, my memory begins to work very well at times like these. Now then, what was the " Oh, Fred " about ?

SALLY (*sulkily*). Nothing. It just slipped out.

CROWTHER. I know it just slipped out. That's why I'm interested in it. What did it mean ?

SALLY. It didn't mean anything.

CROWTHER. We'll see about that. Now then, last night, you went upstairs first—before this other girl, your room-mate, didn't you ?

SALLY. Yes. Because I didn't want to see any more of you.

CROWTHER. I can well believe that. Did you go straight up to your room ?

SALLY. No.

CROWTHER. You didn't, eh ? Well, where did you go ? (*As she does not reply.*) Come on.

EDNA. Really, Mr. Crowther, you must allow us a

little private life. You'll find it on the left at the top of our stairs.

CROWTHER. Oh—all right. Well, once you got into your room, did you stay there ?

SALLY. Yes. You don't expect me to go wandering about all night, do you ?

CROWTHER. No, but that's what a lot of you seem to have been doing. (*Fiercely, to* CLARA.) Was she there when you went in ?

CLARA. Yes.

CROWTHER. And did she stay there ?

CLARA (*after tiny hesitation*). Yes.

CROWTHER (*glaring at her*). What ?

CLARA (*embarrassed and frightened*). Ye-es, I think so.

CROWTHER (*disgusted*). You think so. You're both lying. Well, I'll have the truth.

FRED (*smoothly*). Mr. Crowther, you don't want me again now, do you ?

CROWTHER. You'd better hang on, Fred, because I've asked everybody to come down again. (*Indicating up* R. *above the door.*) You three had better wait there. (*Crossing* R.C. *to* EDNA.) Now I've something to say to you that'll perhaps stop your funny business. Why are you working for the company under a false name ?

EDNA. Have you been searching my room ?

CROWTHER. Yes. I don't like people who lock their rooms and think they're smart because they've got the keys. I found another key you'd overlooked. And then I found a lot of other things too. Including some letters that didn't call you Edna Sandars.

(*Enter* KEITH *and* JORDAN L.)

KEITH. What's this, Crowther ?

CROWTHER. I'm just asking this clever young woman why she works for the company under a false name.

KEITH. What's her real name ?

(*Enter* MISS TRACEY, HELEN *and* MRS. HEATON. *The newcomers must arrange themselves so that both doors are kept clear.*)

CROWTHER (*after waiting for the newcomers to be still*). Her real name's Chennelford. (*He stops, then stares at* EDNA, *triumphantly.*) Chennelford!

EDNA (*quietly*). Yes, you've got it, and I hope you're pleased now. My father was Chennelford, the bank, swindler. He died—in prison—five years ago. I took my mother's name.

(*She backs slowly to the door* R. *and keeps her hands behind her back, so that she can turn the key in the door and then remove the key.*)

CROWTHER. Did the company know it was employing Chennelford's daughter to look after one of its cash desks?

EDNA. No, you'll be able to tell them. It ought to be your big moment. (*She moves across now, towards the other door,* L.)

FRED (*who could see her, sharply*). Here, she's locked that door. (*He moves down to the door, trying it.*)

CROWTHER (*angrily*). Did you?

EDNA. Try it and see.

(*As he takes a step towards the door* R., *very suddenly and quickly she rushes to the door* L., *takes the key out, rushes out and locks it on the other side.*)

CROWTHER (*turning and going across*). Here! She's locking us in. (*He rattles the knob of the door, which is safely locked.*)

MISS TRACEY (*delighted, moving down* O.). Well I never! She seems to be a most enterprising young woman.

(CROWTHER *is at the door* L., *trying it*; FRED *at the door* R., *trying it, and the rest are either looking at the doors or at one another in astonishment—with the exception of* MISS TRACEY, *who is chuckling.*)

BLACK OUT.

ACT III

Same as before. Afternoon.

The door R. is open and remains open now, as it has been forced. Miss Tracey is seated at R. end of the table looking at a small revolver. Clara is standing at up stage R. corner of the table, looking at her. Miss Tracey examines the revolver for a few moments before speaking.

Miss Tracey. Ummm! And you found it up the second flight of stairs, the one leading up to *your* bedroom?

Clara. Yes, Miss Tracey.

Miss Tracey. Did you touch it?

Clara. Well, I couldn't have brought it down here if I hadn't touched it. But I carried it in my apron.

Miss Tracey (*delighted*). Clara, we must examine it for fingerprints.

Clara. Whose?

Miss Tracey (*staring at her thoughtfully*). Whose?

Clara. What's the matter, Miss Tracey?

Miss Tracey (*thoughtfully*). I can't decide if that question of yours is just idiotic or whether it's so terribly sensible that there's no point in looking for the fingerprints. (*She thinks a moment.*) No, we want to find the owner.

Clara. Well, we could ask 'em whose it is.

Miss Tracey (*rather plaintively*). Now don't spoil it, Clara. I *want* to look for fingerprints.

(Clara *picks up the revolver, looking at it, and holds it so that when* Miss Tracey *looks up the barrel it is pointing straight between her eyes.*)

Now if we find it covered with a certain print, that will

be the owner's. Then we've only to make everybody leave their prints—you do it by handing them a glass —I've often read about that—and—— (*She looks up, to see where the revolver is pointing.*) By the way, Clara, if—er—a mouse should run across the floor now—or even if you should happen to sneeze—I believe you'd blow my brains out. Would you mind putting that revolver down?

(CLARA *does so hastily.*)

Now we want some white powder. Face powder would do—probably.

CLARA (*promptly*). Mine's upstairs—and it's pink. Would flour do?

MISS TRACEY. We can try it. Bring a little—in a saucer.

(CLARA *goes out* R.)

But we ought to have a—now what do they call them? I've read about them many a time—an *in- in- insufflator* —yes, that's it—*insufflator*. Sounds ridiculous, but it *is* insufflator.

(CLARA *enters with a saucer of flour and goes back to her former position.*)

Have we got one?

CLARA. One what?

MISS TRACEY. Insufflator.

CLARA (*putting down the saucer*). Never heard of it, Miss Tracey.

MISS TRACEY (*rising*). I'll have to insufflate myself. Now then—you hold it—like that—(*she gives* CLARA *the revolver, flat along her hand*) now turn it up a little— that's right—and I'll take the saucer—(*she takes the saucer and holds it just in front of the revolver—and* CLARA'S *face, for* CLARA *is bending down*) then I blow gently——

(*She does so. Some of the flour goes on to the revolver and a great deal more of it goes on to* CLARA'S *face,*

which was much too near. CLARA sneezes violently.
MISS TRACEY takes the revolver, ignoring CLARA, and
eagerly examines it.)

Humph! This isn't easy—of course we've the other
side of it to do yet, and that may tell us more. But I
can't make much of this. Looks as if it had been
chewed by a dog, which is *quite* ridiculous.

(CLARA *sneezes again, violently.* MISS TRACEY *does not*
look up.)

Don't do that, Clara. *Most* disturbing. I'm afraid
you're not entering into the spirit of this investigation.

(*As she goes on looking, with a white-faced* CLARA *looking*
dumbly on, CROWTHER *enters* L. *He has the hot weary*
look of a completely bewildered and exasperated man.
He comes forward above the table and stares at MISS
TRACEY, *looking at the floury revolver and at the flour-*
covered CLARA, *as if this was the very last straw.*)

(*At last looking up, cheerfully.*) Ah—Mr. Crowther!
How are you getting on?
    CROWTHER (*with a kind of furious patience*). Now
would you mind telling me what you think you're doing?
    MISS TRACEY (*brightly*). Certainly. Looking for
fingerprints.
    CROWTHER (*with furious irony*). Fingerprints! Look
at this! (*Pointing to* CLARA.) And look at this! (*He*
points to the revolver, then recognizes it.) Why, this is *my*
revolver. (*He snatches it up.*) What are you trying to
turn it into—a steak-and-kidney pudding?

(*He blows the flour off in disgust into* CLARA'S *face. She*
sneezes again.)

MISS TRACEY (*coolly*). Well, that's settled, Clara.
It's Mr. Crowther's revolver.
    CLARA (*coolly*). Yes, Miss Tracey.
    CROWTHER (*turning on* CLARA). Will you take this
muck away and then go and wash your face. Fingerprints! And just remember I'm the only detective here.

CLARA (*as she takes the saucer and goes*). And a lot of good *you* are.

(*She goes out* R.)

CROWTHER. And there's something for you to remember too, Miss Tracey. A woman came to this hotel last night, and she's disappeared, probably been murdered. Just remember that, while you're having your fun, just remember that.

MISS TRACEY. I know. (*She replaces her chair between the radio and the sideboard.*) You keep telling us to remember it. But there's something about that woman, Mrs. Jernigan, that makes it impossible to keep remembering her. I thought so, last night. (*She breaks off, then resumes briskly.*) Well, have you found that girl, Edna Sandars ?

CROWTHER (*in disgust*). No, and if she's in this hotel, then I'm going blind. This place is enough to drive a man barmy. First, this Mrs. Jernigan disappears—and out of a room with every door locked inside and every window fastened. Now this girl gives herself five minutes' start by locking us in here—and then completely disappears too. I've been four solid hours looking for her. (*Working down* L.) Not a trace. Clean gone. Well, where ? And where's Mrs. Jernigan, dead or alive ? What is this—an hotel or an Egyptian Palace of Mysteries on Blackpool Sands ?

MISS TRACEY (*up* R.). Which question do you want me to answer first ?

CROWTHER (*disgustedly*). Any of 'em.

MISS TRACEY (*brightly*). Then, I think it must be an Egyptian Palace of Mysteries.

CROWTHER. Oh——

(*He breaks off as* KEITH *enters* R. *wearing his overcoat. He has obviously just been out.*)

Now where have you been ?

KEITH. Outside.

CROWTHER (*belligerently—crossing to him*). You didn't ask *my* permission to go out.

KEITH. No, why should I ?

CROWTHER (*same tone*). Because I'm still in charge here—until the police come—and I can't have people who are under suspicion going where they like.

KEITH. But, Crowther, surely you don't suspect *me* ?

CROWTHER. Don't I ? Well, explain that—— (*He produces a small piece of paper, and holds it out.*)

KEITH (*reading it*). What is it ? Something—something—" Rue Morny, Algiers." (*To* CROWTHER, *bewildered.*) What does it mean ?

CROWTHER. Of course you've never seen it before, have you ?

KEITH. No. It doesn't mean anything to me.

CROWTHER. It was in your room. And I'll tell you another thing. *Another* bit of paper—with the same address on it—" Rue Morny, Algiers "—was found on the floor of Mrs. Jernigan's room, last night.

(KEITH *is silent, rather dazed by this information.* MISS TRACEY *comes down to above the table.*)

Now do you understand why I can't allow you to go where you like ?

KEITH (*quietly*). Yes. I think that's quite reasonable, Crowther. You'll find me here whenever you want me.

CROWTHER (*ungraciously*). All right. That's better.

MISS TRACEY. I think we agreed this morning, Mr. Crowther, that anybody could have put that bit of paper in Mr. Henley's room. There was plenty of opportunity.

KEITH. Thank you, Miss Tracey.

CROWTHER (*mocking* KEITH). Yes, thank you, Miss Tracey. And now, Miss Tracey, just listen to me. I'm getting tired of your interference, and I'm beginning to tumble to it. And if there's any more of it—I'm going to take a chance—and have you confined to your room —until the police come—and if you'll take my advice you'll go to your room now——

MISS TRACEY (*coolly*). I haven't the least intention of taking your advice, Mr. Crowther. (*She sits in the chair above the table* o.)

CROWTHER (*after glaring at* MISS TRACEY, *he turns to* KEITH). What did you go out for ?

KEITH. You may not have noticed it, but it's been thawing for the last few hours. I wanted to see if we were still snowed in here.

MISS TRACEY. Are we ?

KEITH. No, I think the road's reasonably clear. And somebody else must have thought so too.

CROWTHER. That girl ?

KEITH. Yes, it must have been Edna Sandars. Everybody else is still here.

CROWTHER (*excitedly*). You sure ?

KEITH. Go and see for yourself. The tracks are there, quite new. And one of the cars is missing.

CROWTHER. Whose ?

KEITH. Yours.

CROWTHER (*astounded, furious*). What ! My car ?

KEITH. 'Fraid so, Crowther. She must have escaped in your car.

CROWTHER (*furious*). The little—— (*He does not say the horrid word.*) That settles her—and the whole case. But I'll make sure.

(*He hurries out* R.)

MISS TRACEY. That clears you, then. Because even Crowther, who seems to me one of the very stupidest men I've ever met, could hardly believe that you and this girl, Edna Sandars, committed a crime together. You don't like her, do you ?

KEITH (*dubiously*). Well—she's not the type—I care for—certainly. We weren't getting on very well together, because she was far too cheeky—and I'd had to tick her off several times because she was so rude to Miss Tennant.

MISS TRACEY (*thoughtfully*). Yes, I can imagine that.

KEITH. But still—I don't like to think—somehow—she was mixed up in this horrible business. Though of course she must have been.

MISS TRACEY (*thoughtfully*). I think she knows more

about it than any of you. (*She looks at* Keith.) A pity, eh?

Keith (*slowly, distastefully*). Yes—I can't help feeling sorry—somehow.

(*Enter* Jordan l. *He is agitated.*)

Jordan. Crowther asked me to see him here again. More questions. Why? Why? Why? And I have nothing—nothing—nothing—to tell him. (*Down* l.)

Miss Tracey. Mr. Henley, will you do something for me?

Keith (*up to her*). Certainly, Miss Tracey.

Miss Tracey. Go at once to Mrs. Heaton and tell her that Mr. Jordan is about to be arrested. (*As* Keith *hesitates, puzzled.*) It's not a joke. Please go.

(*He exits* l.)

Jordan. So you have found out? It is you who ought to be the detective.

Miss Tracey. I've always wanted to be one, but I'm afraid it's too late now—

Jordan (*at* l. *bottom corner of the table*). But no—you are still young—you have energy—you have enthusiasm —you have the acuteness——

Miss Tracey (*rising*). Mr. Jordan, for those idiotic but perfectly delightful words, I shall make you a happy man. Have you a toothbrush?

Jordan. I have three toothbrushes.

Miss Tracey. Could you pack the three toothbrushes?

Jordan. But why?

Miss Tracey. To run away—with your wife. That is, if you still love her.

Jordan (*with immense enthusiasm, crossing* r. *and back to* l.c.). Miss Tracey, I adore that woman. She is all wrong. She is too quiet, she is too determined, she is too critical, too fault-finding. But I adore her. She is a statue, a stone, a piece of ice——

(Mrs. Heaton *enters* l. *almost at a run.*)

MRS. HEATON. Oh—Arnold—Arnold! (*She flings herself into his arms.*)

JORDAN. My love—my angel!

MRS. HEATON (*almost weeping*). They shan't touch you.

JORDAN. With you, I am invincible.

(*As they are still looking fondly at each other,* CLARA *enters* R. *She gives them one startled look.*)

CLARA. Oo—er!

MISS TRACEY (*with authority, moving* R.C.). Yes, you can go, Clara. (*As* CLARA *goes.*) Mr. Jordan. The toothbrushes. Hers too, eh? And hurry.

JORDAN. Yes. (*To* MRS. HEATON.) My love, I must go—but only for a few minutes—then we will never be parted again.

(*He hurries out* R., *leaving his wife staring after him. She turns to* MISS TRACEY.)

MRS. HEATON. Is he in danger?

MISS TRACEY (*sitting* R. *by the small table*). No. And I'm surprised at you, Mrs. Jordan. Why did you quarrel with such a delightful husband, who adores you?

MRS. HEATON. It was all my fault. (*Crossing to her.*) We were married secretly—because of business. Then, we got leave at the same time, and went away—it was really our honeymoon. And then almost at once we quarrelled. He was angry with me.

MISS TRACEY (*severely*). I would have thought a woman like you would have been able to manage him, even if he was angry with you. Why didn't you make him specially comfortable—cook tasty little meals for him?

MRS. HEATON. How could I when he's a chef?

MISS TRACEY. What did you quarrel about?

MRS. HEATON. There was a competition for a new sweet. He had invented one—and he had called it Tangerine Rose—as a compliment to me——

MISS TRACEY. And very nice too. Nobody's ever called anything after me. What was it made of?

MRS. HEATON. Slices of tangerine oranges—vanilla ice cream—with a chocolate sauce. He made some for me. And I—(*almost tearfully*) I said it was sickly.

MISS TRACEY. It sounds sickly to me.

MRS. HEATON (*indignantly*). It isn't. It's beautiful. Everybody likes it. And then——

MISS TRACEY. I know. You quarrelled. Then you both came here, and he couldn't find your room and went knocking everybody up. Now the only thing for you to do is to take him away—anywhere—and make a fuss of him. (*Taking* MRS. HEATON *by the shoulders and moving her towards the door* R.) That's why I've told him to go and pack a few things. Yours and his.

MRS. HEATON (*gasping*). But Mr. Crowther wouldn't let us go.

MISS TRACEY. Dodge him. I'll take the responsibility afterwards. You have a car, I suppose?

MRS. HEATON. Arnold has.

MISS TRACEY. Good. Well, you'll run into snowdrifts, and one of you will probably catch pneumonia and nearly die, but that'll all help.

MRS. HEATON. I'll risk it. But why are you doing all this?

MISS TRACEY. Because the pair of you, mooning round, are just in the way here. And because I'd like to see you happy.

MRS. HEATON. I'm ready, if Arnold is. And, Miss Tracey, I don't know how to thank you.

MISS TRACEY (*hurriedly*). Your husband must cook me a nice dinner some time, that'll do. But no " Tangerine Rose "—it sounds horribly sickly—just a cheese soufflé. Now Crowther is outside, where the cars are. Get ready, and when he comes in, you dodge out. Off you go.

(MRS. HEATON *hurries out* R. MISS TRACEY *takes out a small notebook and makes a note in it.* SALLY *enters* L. *She looks very unhappy, as if she had been crying. She walks slowly above the table to* R.C. *without looking at* MISS TRACEY, *who, however, looks curiously at her.*)

Let me see—you're Sally, aren't you ?

SALLY (*sulkily*). Yes. What do you want ?

MISS TRACEY (*briskly, with authority*). Come, come, come, Sally, that's no way to talk. And no way to look, either. What have you been crying about ?

SALLY (*defiantly*). Who says I've been crying ?

MISS TRACEY. I do. Now listen to me, my dear. (*She goes up to her.*) I know I'm not one of the staff. I'm a guest. But you mustn't regard me as a guest. You can say just what you like to me.

SALLY (*her interest awaking*). So you're a guest I can say just what I like to ?

MISS TRACEY. Yes.

SALLY (*with growing fierceness*). Well, I've always wanted to find one. Guests ! I've had to do with 'em for ten years, and they make me sick. Yes—sick ! Guests ! Visitors ! Patrons ! Whatever you want to call yourselves. You aren't 'uman. You're not. I wouldn't have believed there was such people, if I hadn't let myself in for ten years of you. (*She breaks off.*)

MISS TRACEY (*with cheerful interest*). Don't stop. What's the matter with us ?

SALLY. · Everything. To start with, you don't know anything—like a lot o' babies. (*Mimicking them.*) Oh —where do I find this ? How do I find that ? Where's the dining-room, where's the bar, where's my daughter, where's my husband ? How do I get out ? I want to wash my hands, I want to blow my nose. And look at the mess you make ! Just because you haven't to tidy it up ! As soon as you get into a bedroom, you've got it all turned upside down, as if there'd been a lot of drunk elephants in the place. Spilling face-powder ! Leaving your clothes anywhere ! And what you do with the towels, God only knows ! Just like a lot o' barmy babies !

MISS TRACEY (*with the same cheerful tone*). Thank you, my dear. I must say I don't recognize myself in all this, but I'm glad to know what goes on in the heads of chambermaids.

SALLY (*sulky again now*). Well, that's only some of

it. And it's done me good to get that bit out. And
if you'd like to have me sacked, you can do, because
I'm fed up anyhow. (*Miserably.*) I don't care what
happens now.

MISS TRACEY (*slowly moving down* R.). I see. Well,
there are only four men here. I think I can rule out
Mr. Crowther and Mr. Jordan. That leaves Mr. Henley
and that young man who's so pleased with himself,
Fred. Mr. Henley is an attractive young man, but I
don't think you'd consider yourself at liberty to cry
over him. So it must be Fred. Now what has Fred
done ?

(*But at this moment* CROWTHER *enters* R.)

CROWTHER. She's gone all right and my car with
her. *And*—for all we know—anything that's left of
Mrs. Jernigan.

MISS TRACEY. Do you believe that this girl, Edna
Sandars——

CROWTHER. Chennelford. Don't forget her real
name. Daughter of a crook.

MISS TRACEY. Sandars or Chennelford, it doesn't
matter.

(SALLY *moves slowly across and down* L.)

But do you believe that this girl was capable of killing
Mrs. Jernigan, spiriting her body out of a locked room,
hiding it for a night and half a day, and then taking it
down to a car outside ?

CROWTHER. Yes, with a bit of help perhaps. Suppose the body was pushed out of a window——

SALLY (*with horror*). Oo—for Gawd's sake—stop it.
The *body* !

CROWTHER. If you don't like it, don't listen. (*Crossing up stage to* C. *and speaking to* MISS TRACEY.) If
the road's open, they may have repaired the telephone
line. I'll try the police.

MISS TRACEY. You needn't. They're on their way.

CROWTHER. D'you mean to say you——

MISS TRACEY. They rang us up to see if we were all

right. I told them what had happened and they said
they'd send some men out. They asked if the room had
been sealed up. (*Following him to* c.) I said I didn't
think it had.

CROWTHER. It hasn't, either. (*Moving out towards
the door* L., *saying, almost to himself :*) Better see what
it's looking like.

(*He goes out hurriedly.*)

SALLY (*coolly*). Mind you, Miss Tracey, the more
lies anybody tells that Crowther, the better I'll be
pleased. So don't think I'm complaining. But I would
like to know what the idea is.

MISS TRACEY. Don't you believe the police *did* telephone ?

SALLY (*coolly*). I know very well they didn't. I've
just spent ten minutes myself with that telephone and
it's as dead as ever it was. So if you didn't want him
to telephone, you needn't have told him that little
fairy-tale. But why don't *you* want him to tell the
police about all this ?

MISS TRACEY. Because I'm on the point of discover-
ing something, and I think that Crowther and the police
between them would spoil everything.

SALLY (*crossing to the door* R.). I believe you.

MISS TRACEY. Well, now give me a chance of be-
lieving something *you* say. What has that barman,
Fred, done that you should cry over it ? (*As she does
not reply.*) Is he—your young man ? (*As she does not
reply.*) Sally, I am not interested in your private affairs.

SALLY. You sound interested enough.

MISS TRACEY. No. It's not that. But I must know
exactly what's been happening here, and what the
relations are between all you people.

SALLY (*half defiant, half contemptuous*). Oh—*you* must ?

MISS TRACEY. That's what I said.

SALLY (*up to* R.C. *of the table*). You come when
the hotel's not open—we let you stay the night—then
the trouble begins—and now you say you have to know
this and that and the other—what everybody thinks

about everybody else—and God knows what.   Haven't
you got a nerve, Miss Tracey?

MISS TRACEY.   Yes, I have.   You're perfectly right.
Where you're wrong is in thinking I arrived here by
accident.   I came here for the express purpose of find-
ing out about all you people.   Now then—you're obviously in love with that young barman.   How long has
it been going on?

SALLY.   It hasn't been going on.   Fred was working
at the same hotel as me three years ago, and we were
very good friends then.   I've been kidding myself we'd
be good friends again up here, but it seems I'm wrong.
Fred's got grand ideas now.   That comes of being in the
cocktail bar, pouring out gins for these society girls.

MISS TRACEY.   I see.   The trouble is, you're not such
good friends now because Fred has grand ideas.   You've
just told him so?

SALLY.   Yes.   And he didn't like it.   Turned on me.

MISS TRACEY.   Because you saw him last night, eh?

SALLY (*startled*).   Who told you?

(*A pause, then* FRED *strolls in* L., *humming a little tune.
He gives* SALLY *and* MISS TRACEY *a quick look.*)

FRED.   Just heard we're not snowed in any longer.
That right, Miss Tracey?

MISS TRACEY.   I believe so.

FRED.   Hello, Sally.   How's things?

SALLY (*in a muffled tone*).   You know.

(*She walks off quickly* R.   FRED *looks after her and
whistles, then gives* MISS TRACEY *a droll look.*)

FRED.   Nice girl, but temperamental.   (*To* L.C. *lower
corner of the table.*)   That's her trouble.   Won't take it
easy.   Now I believe in taking it easy.   Have to in
my job, Miss Tracey.

MISS TRACEY (*rather gaily*).   I'm sure you have.   And
that reminds me.   Would you like to do an old woman
a great favour?   (*She comes to* R.C. *corner of the table.*)

FRED.   Delighted, Miss Tracey.

MISS TRACEY.   I don't care for cocktails myself—I
prefer a little dry sherry—but some of my friends like

them, and I'm told you've invented a wonderful cocktail called the " Silver Queen." Now is it a secret ?

FRED (*smiling*). It was, but it isn't now. Do you
want to know how to make it ? (*Coming* c.)

MISS TRACEY (*pleased*). Yes, if you don't mind.

FRED (*beginning rather quickly*). Take one part of
orange-juice, one part of lemon-juice, then——

MISS TRACEY (*breaking in*). I'm sorry, but I shan't
possibly remember. Would you mind putting it down
for me, please ? (*She hands him a sheet from her notebook and a pencil.*)

FRED. Certainly, Miss Tracey. (*As he writes—more
or less under his breath.*) One of orange—one of lemon
. . . (*He then becomes more or less inaudible as he writes
the cocktail.*)

MISS TRACEY (*as he continues writing*). Oranges and
lemons ! Dear me, it doesn't sound as exhilarating as I
had hoped.

FRED (*handing back the sheet and the pencil*). There
you are, Miss Tracey. And don't let 'em have too
many. It's stronger than it looks.

MISS TRACEY (*gushing, rather*). I'm *most* obliged.
" Silver Queen." Such a charming name, too ! Now I
must be very careful with this. (*She moves away* R.)

(*She puts it in her notebook and puts the notebook in her
pocket with great care. FRED gives her a glance of
contempt, which instantly changes to his usual bright
smile when she looks up again. KEITH enters L., looking
rather miserable.*)

FRED. Mr. Henley, I'd like to get away some time
to-day if I could.

KEITH. It's no use asking me, Fred.

FRED. But you're in charge, Mr. Henley ?

KEITH. No, I'm simply one of the suspects. (*Crossing* R. *above the table.*) You'll have to ask Crowther.
As far as I'm concerned, Fred, you can go.

FRED. Thanks. I'll see if I can square it with
Crowther. He knows I'd nothing to do with this
business. Couldn't have.

(*He goes out* L.   MISS TRACEY *looks hard at* KEITH, *who is looking gloomier than ever.*)

MISS TRACEY.   What is it, young man ?

KEITH.   Everything.   Crowther says the police are on their way up here, and I've just realized what a mess I'm in.   I'd nothing to do with it, of course, though Crowther seems to think I have.   But whatever happens, I can say good-bye to this job—and the company.

MISS TRACEY.   Oh—come now !

KEITH.   I'm not blaming you, Miss Tracey.   But that woman oughtn't to have been staying here at all.   At least one of my staff here—Edna Sandars—will be arrested.   There'll be yards of stuff in the papers.   Head Office will be furious.   Then—good-bye !   I'm being very selfish, I suppose, worrying about myself and my job, when we don't even know what's become of that poor old girl—but—you see, Miss Tracey—the hotel business isn't just a job to me.   I've never wanted to do anything else.   And I've worked like a nigger—ever since I left school—to get as far as I have done.   And now—I'm through.

MISS TRACEY (*calmly*).   Nonsense !

KEITH.   Oh—you don't know.

MISS TRACEY.   On the contrary, I *do* know—and you don't.   To begin with, the police *aren't* on their way here.   That's just one of my little jokes with poor Mr. Crowther.

KEITH (*surprised*).   But why——?

MISS TRACEY (*cutting in quickly, lowering her voice*).   You must take my word for this.   The telephone isn't through yet, but it may be at any moment.   Now if you want to keep your job, you must see that the police don't come here.

KEITH (*surprised, shocked*).   But I couldn't——

MISS TRACEY (*cutting in quickly again*).   Yes, you could.   Listen for the telephone, they're sure to ring through when they've repaired the line.   See that you answer it yourself.   If that fool Crowther answers it, there'll be endless trouble. Now remember—no police, no reporters. Then you're all right.

KEITH. But we can't hush this up?

MISS TRACEY (*calmly*). Yes, we can.

KEITH. What! A woman disappears——

MISS TRACEY (*cutting in*). You're beginning to talk like Crowther. Stop it. Just do what I tell you—and trust me. (*She breaks off, then in a bright, social tone.*) Do you know, Mr. Henley, I haven't enjoyed myself so much for years.

(*While he is still staring at her* HELEN TENNANT *enters* L. *She is wearing a little winter hat and a heavy coat, perhaps a fur coat—not fastened—and she is carrying a black handbag. She looks very charming. She smiles at* KEITH.)

HELEN (*up stage* C.). Oh—Mr. Henley—I've been looking for you. (*She smiles at him again. She conveys to* MISS TRACEY *the fact that* MISS TRACEY *is now in the way.*)

MISS TRACEY (*rather sweetly*). A little business talk, no doubt?

HELEN (*sweetly*). Yes—if you don't mind?

MISS TRACEY. I was just going. I want to see what Crowther's doing with that fatal room. (*She crosses to the door* L. *below the table, then turns.*) Now remember, Mr. Henley.

(*She goes.*)

HELEN (*raising her eyebrows*). Remember what—Keith? (*Crossing to him—charmingly.*) You don't mind my calling you Keith, do you?

KEITH. Rather not. I'm all for it—Helen.

HELEN (*smiling*). Good! What have you to remember? Or is it a secret?

KEITH. Well—she's being rather mysterious—I don't make her out.

HELEN (*appealingly*). Is that all—Keith?

KEITH. Well—no. As a matter of fact, she wants to try and keep the police out of this.

HELEN. Really? But she can't do that. Crowther just told me they're on their way here now.

KEITH (*confidentially*). No, they're not. She told Crowther that. Actually, the telephone isn't through yet.

HELEN (*slowly*). Oh! Now—I wonder what difference that will make to me. (*With charming, confidential tone.*) Keith, now that the road's open, I'd like to get away as soon as I decently can. There are a lot of things I have to do in town—more than I thought now I've seen the hotel—and I would like to be getting on with the job. You see, Keith—I'm like you—really keen and excited about what I can do here.

KEITH (*shyly*). I know you are, Helen. It's one of the things—just one of the things—I like about you— admire you for.

HELEN (*archly*). You be careful.

KEITH (*fatuously*). I don't want to be careful.

HELEN. You're beginning to sound like a very dangerous young man. But—(*with a change of tone, rather burlesqued*) to business, Mr. Henley. I don't know anything about this horrid affair here. Even Mr. Crowther admits that. I've lots of things I ought to be doing. I'll leave an address, of course—I'm not going to run away. So—please—when may I go?

KEITH. Well—Crowther's in charge, you know, until the police *do* come.

HELEN. Yes, but you represent the company, Keith. Now as far as you're concerned——?

KEITH. You're at liberty to go whenever you want to go. And I'll do my best to see that it's as soon as possible. (*With a more personal tone.*) And that's very noble of me, you know, Helen. I know I'll hate your going.

HELEN. Oh—but I'll be back very soon. Then we'll be here—both of us—for the whole season.

KEITH (*rather gloomily*). I hope so.

HELEN (*gaily*). But of course.

KEITH. Oh—you'll be all right. I'm not so sure about me.

(FRED *enters* L. *He is wearing an overcoat, but is not carrying a hat.*)

FRED. Oh—excuse me, Mr. Henley.

KEITH. What is it, Fred ?

FRED (*smoothly, coming* C. *below the table*). I've just heard there's a chance of Miss Tennant getting away soon. Is that right, Miss Tennant ?

HELEN. I'm hoping to. Why ?

FRED. Well—I must get back to London as soon as I can. I told you, Mr. Henley, I just looked in because I knew they wouldn't have ordered all the stuff I want, and the only thing is for me to do it myself. So I wondered, Miss Tennant, if it isn't too much to ask, if you'd kindly give me a lift in your car. (*Humbly.*) It would be a great convenience.

HELEN. Why, yes, of course I will.

FRED. Thank you very much, Miss Tennant. Is that all right to you, Mr. Henley ?

KEITH. Yes, naturally. Though of course I don't know when exactly you'll both be able to go.

FRED. No. But Mr. Crowther knows I'm all right. I never even saw the old lady. I was in bed before she turned up. And I have my work to do, as you know, Mr. Henley. That American Bar will be open—and probably doing big business over Easter—in less than a fortnight.

KEITH (*rather gloomily*). Let's hope so.

HELEN (*to* FRED). Our assistant manager is a bit gloomy this afternoon.

FRED (*briskly*). Now then, Mr. Henley. (*Crossing* HELEN *to* KEITH.) Don't you start worrying——

(*He is interrupted by the entrance* R. *of* EDNA. *She should be wearing a rather bulky winter coat, not closely buttoned, and she should keep one hand pressed to her side. She is wearing a small cloche hat, which on entering she plucks off and flings carelessly down.*)

EDNA (*coolly*). Well, well, well !

(*She stands or leans near the door, looking quizzically at them, as they stare in amazement at her.*)

If we aren't in conference !

FRED (*going up* R.).   I didn't expect to see *you* again.

EDNA.   Too bad, Fred.

HELEN (*calmly, leaning quietly against bottom* R. *corner of the table*).   I hope you've brought the police back with you.

EDNA.   Do you know, I clean forgot.   Stupid of me !

KEITH (*thunderstruck*).   This beats me.   Why did you go away ?   Why have you come back ?

EDNA (*shaking her head*).   Just a whimsical little girl, that's me, Mr. Henley.   Nothing but a bundle of fads and fancies.   Nothing——

KEITH (*crossly interrupting*).   Oh—drop it !   (*He goes up* C. *above the table*.)

EDNA.   Right.   (*Looking sharply at* HELEN *and* FRED.)   All ready dressed for the road, eh ?   (*She moves forward slowly, towards* HELEN.)   Leaving us so soon, Miss Tennant ?   And just when we poor members of the lower classes were beginning to admire you.   *And* your very handsome bag.

(*She suddenly snatches the bag from* HELEN'S *grasp, and sticks it under her big coat as she sharply retreats towards the door* R.)

HELEN (*angrily*).   Give me that bag, you fool !

(*She goes after her, but* FRED *is quicker and comes down between* EDNA *and the door*.)

FRED (*sharply, with a very different tone from his usual one*).   All right, I'll handle this.   That bag—quick !   (*Holding out his hand*.)   Come on.   Or I'll flatten you.   (*Looking very menacing*.)   That bag.

(*There is a pause*.)

EDNA.   Oh—all right.

(*She produces a duplicate bag from under her coat.*   FRED *snatches it away*.)

FRED (*moving back to his former position up stage* R.).   I'll take care of this, if you like, Miss Tennant—until——   (*He looks at her significantly*.)

HELEN. All right, thank you, Fred. (*Severely to* EDNA, *moving towards the door* R.) You must be crazy. It's the only possible explanation.

(*She goes out* R. *The others watch her go.*)

KEITH (*helplessly*). I suppose I'd better tell Crowther. He's the only person who can deal with this. (*He is still* C.)

EDNA. Don't call me " this." It's rude.

KEITH. I'd like to know what on earth you can be called.

EDNA (*with mock fatuousness*). Just—Edna. And I'll bet you've been calling that nice Miss Tennant " Helen," haven't you ? Now, don't blush.

FRED. Completely off her nut, she is !

EDNA (*to* KEITH, *crossing to the table*). Shall I tell you what dear Helen is doing now, while you're standing there, covered with tender blushes ? She's just nipped out to see if her car's all ready——

FRED (*growling*). All right, we know all about it.

EDNA (*seriously now, to* KEITH). Keith Henley, you can't say I didn't warn you. It's nearly too late, but not quite. Now don't be a fool.

KEITH. Oh—be quiet.

FRED (*menacingly, coming down* R. *of her*). I'll soon keep her quiet.

EDNA (*lightly but seriously*). Is that all right, Keith ? Fred means it. He'd keep me quiet. I can see it in his eye. Do you mind ?

FRED (*making a step towards her*). I'd just like to give you——

KEITH (*sharply*). No. Drop it, Fred. (*As* FRED *does not move and still looks menacing.*) Come away. Leave her alone.

(FRED *steps back reluctantly.* EDNA *looks at him, then at* KEITH.)

EDNA (*quietly*). Thanks, Keith. You're a fool, but a nice fool. (*She comes a little down stage, then turns to them with her back to the audience.*) And even you

ought to have noticed by now that our cheerful little
Fred has suddenly changed character. That's because
he knows the game's up. Don't you, Fred ?

(EDNA *stares at* FRED, *who is glowering at her.* KEITH
looks from one to the other of them, puzzled, frowning.
CROWTHER *now bursts in* L., *and comes down* L.C.)

CROWTHER (*heatedly*). That damn telephone *isn't*
working—— (*He catches sight of* EDNA *and stops in
amazement.*) What, you !

EDNA (*brightly*). And a merry, merry Christmas, Mr.
Crowther !

CROWTHER (*roaring*). Where's my car ?

EDNA (*coolly*). Outside, what's left of it. You don't
deserve to have a car, Crowther, the way you look after
it. There and back—knocking all the time—like a
postman.

CROWTHER (*striding forward, in a towering rage*).
Sandars or Chennelford or whatever your name is—you
can consider yourself under arrest.

EDNA (*impudently*). All right. And you can consider yourself a real detective. And what shall we turn
them (*indicating* KEITH *and* FRED) into—Aladdin and
Puss-in-Boots ? And now we'll all have a nice game.

CROWTHER. You'll have that all right. (*Moving
towards her.*) The minute the police are here, you'll
be under arrest. (*He turns to* KEITH.) Where's Jordan ?

KEITH. Don't ask me.

CROWTHER (*exasperated*). Does anybody know anything here ? (*Crossing* EDNA *slowly towards the door* R.)
That mad woman upstairs goes and tells me that the
police rang up, and now it seems the 'phone hasn't
been working yet.

(*As soon as he has crossed her* EDNA *has moved across* L.
above the table to the chair L. *of the table. As he turns
slowly round at the door as if thinking, he catches sight
of her apparently on her way out* L.)

(*Coming a step away from the door* R.) Here, what are
you doing ?

EDNA (*as she sits*). Sitting down.

(*As* CROWTHER *is glaring at her and everybody else, and mopping his brow,* HELEN *enters* R. *and stands just above the door. She looks quickly at* FRED *and nods.*)

FRED. All right out there, eh, Miss Tennant?

HELEN. Yes. And how is it in here?

FRED (*slowly and significantly*). Not so good.

CROWTHER (*suspiciously*). What do you mean—*not so good*?

EDNA. He's telling her that I've tumbled to him.

CROWTHER (*angrily*). Will you shut your mouth?

EDNA. And will you open your mind? Just think a minute now, even if it kills you.

(CROWTHER *goes over to the door* R. *and stands in front of it. Of the other four,* HELEN *and* FRED *stand the nearest to him.*)

CROWTHER (*firmly*). Now then, Fred, just tell me what you meant then, will you?

FRED (*smoothly*). Why, Mr. Crowther, just what I said, that things aren't so good in here—everybody getting in a temper—you know.

CROWTHER. I see.

KEITH. I don't. He meant something more than that.

EDNA. Hello, are *you* coming at last out of the chloroform?

CROWTHER (*shouting*). Will you be quiet?

(MISS TRACEY *enters briskly* L. *and looks astonished and delighted at the scene she finds.*)

MISS TRACEY. Well now! (*Coming down* L.) This looks like business, doesn't it? (*She sees* EDNA.) Ah— so you're back, Miss Sandars.

EDNA. Yes, back in the dear old place, Miss Tracey.

CROWTHER (*shouting across at* MISS TRACEY). Heigh, just a minute!

MISS TRACEY (*now standing down* L.). You're not addressing me, are you?

EDNA (*quickly*). No, he's calling a taxi.

CROWTHER. Yes, I'm talking to you. Do you know anything about Jordan—and that woman—Mrs. Heaton ?

MISS TRACEY. Oh—haven't you been able to find them ?

CROWTHER. No, I haven't.

MISS TRACEY (*pleased*). Then they've gone. I told them to go.

CROWTHER (*angrily*). *You* told them ! Now that just puts the lid on it. (*He comes forward a step.*)

EDNA (*urgently*). No, stay there, Crowther. It's important. Don't move.

(*Arrested by her tone, CROWTHER still occupies the doorway. MISS TRACEY now suddenly produces a small revolver from her pocket and points it at them all.*)

MISS TRACEY (*sharply*). Don't move, anybody. It's about time I took charge.

(*They are all silent, covered by the revolver. MISS TRACEY suddenly looks delighted.*)

D'you know, I've always wanted to do this. *Most* satisfactory !

EDNA. Well, I'm on your side—but I wish you'd put it away.

FRED (*speaking from the side of his mouth, to HELEN*). Be ready !

EDNA (*hastily warning*). Watch them, Crowther.

CROWTHER (*urgently*). Drop that gun.

KEITH. Miss Tracey, for God's sake—be careful !

MISS TRACEY (*still covering them*). I must confess I don't find this very comfortable—nor conducive to rational conversation. And it's about time we had a little rational conversation. One moment.

(*The revolver, tiring to hold, has been weighing down her arm. She now transfers it to the other hand.*)

FRED (*shouting*). Look out !

(*They all duck and at the same time, startled by the shout,*

CROWTHER *disappears through the door behind him.*
MISS TRACEY *involuntarily pulls the trigger, the revolver
goes off with a very loud report, well above their heads.
They remain ducking.* MISS TRACEY *throws the revolver down. Everybody gives an audible sigh of relief
and gradually assumes upright posture.* FRED *and*
HELEN, *on getting up, exchange places, so that* FRED
is R. *and* HELEN R.C. *Just as they do this the door* L.
slowly opens and the scared faces of SALLY *and* CLARA
*look in. Their eyes travel round the room, noting that
nobody is killed. Then, with droll haste, they disappear
and shut the door.* KEITH *picks up the revolver.*)

MISS TRACEY. Ridiculous thing!

CROWTHER (*peeping cautiously through the door, mopping his brow, then coming just inside—to* KEITH). Give
me that gun! (*To* MISS TRACEY.) It's my belief—
and I'm ready to declare it on oath—that you're clean
off your head. (*Explosively.*) Dotty!

MISS TRACEY. Well, I really must apologize for this
revolver business—I see now it was all wrong—just as I
was ready to take charge, too.

HELEN (*sweetly*). Mr. Crowther, now that the excitement's over, I'd like to go—please. (*She moves down to*
R. *corner of the table.*)

CROWTHER. Here, wait a minute, I didn't say you
could go yet.

FRED (*slowly moving down to* CROWTHER). And I'd
like to go too, Mr. Crowther.

CROWTHER (*involuntarily backing into the doorway as*
FRED *moves nearer*). Now, just a minute, Fred——

FRED (*softly*). But you said it would be all right,
Mr. Crowther—— (*He moves nearer, slowly.*)

CROWTHER. Not yet, Fred. Keep still.

EDNA (*rising sharply*). Watch him!

FRED (*yelling*). Come on.

(*This is to* HELEN, *who is close behind him. At the same
time he jumps forward, and as* CROWTHER *retreats into
the doorway,* FRED *knocks him out.* CROWTHER *falls
through the door, so that only his legs are visible to the*

audience. FRED, *followed closely by* HELEN, *hurries
off* R. *We hear* FRED *shouting*—"Straight down
here"—*off stage.* KEITH *hurries off* R., *obviously to
attend to* CROWTHER. EDNA *and* MISS TRACEY *go to
the doorway.*)

KEITH (*just off*). You all right, Crowther?
EDNA (*looking off, down*). He's out.

(MISS TRACEY *crosses to the other door* L., *opens it and
calls.*)

MISS TRACEY. Sally. Clara. (*She comes back again
to down* L.)
EDNA (*still looking out*). Poor old Crowther! But
he'll be all right soon. You couldn't hurt that head.
Solid ivory!
MISS TRACEY. No chance of stopping those two, I
suppose?
EDNA. No, she had her car all ready. It doesn't
matter.

(*Enter* SALLY *and* CLARA *wonderingly.*)

SALLY (*crossing to* C. *above the table*). What's up?
MISS TRACEY (*briskly*). Mr. Crowther's been knocked
out.
SALLY. Who did it?
EDNA. Fred.
SALLY. Well, I'm not surprised.
MISS TRACEY (*briskly*). Now you two girls attend to
him, and help Mr. Henley.
CLARA (*dazed*). What do we do?
MISS TRACEY. Oh—vinegar and brown paper and all
that sort of thing. (*Calling.*) Mr. Henley, do you
know what to do?
KEITH (*appearing at the door*). I think so. I used to
do some boxing.
EDNA (*interested*). Did you? Why didn't you tell
me before?
KEITH (*to* SALLY *and* CLARA). Give me a hand, you
two.

(KEITH *takes* CROWTHER'S *shoulders,* SALLY *and* CLARA *a leg each, and they carry him out.*)

SALLY (*as she goes*).   He can have all the vinegar he wants from me.

MISS TRACEY (*to* EDNA, *as soon as they are alone*). You knew—about those two ?

EDNA.   Yes.

MISS TRACEY.   Unfortunately, we haven't much evidence.   That's why it's a pity they got away like that.

EDNA.   We've more evidence than you think—unless I'm greatly mistaken.   We'll have a look at this.

(*She now produces from her coat the bag she took from* HELEN, *and puts it on the table, also takes off her coat and puts it over the chair to one side* R.   *She then sits on* R. *end of the table.*   MISS TRACEY *sits in the chair* C. *below the table.*)

Helen Tennant's bag.   She thinks Fred has it.   But the one Fred is carrying—I bought it three hours ago—is full of paper and stones.   There ought to be something juicier than that in this one.

(EDNA *opens it, taking out a handkerchief, compact, small purse, etc., and then some letters.   They look at the letters.*)

You see.   "Rue Morny, Algiers."   Wait !   Look at this.   Gives you the whole scheme.   (*They look at the letter, which is small and in pencil.*)   No signature, though.   (*Reading.*)   "When I see you up there." That's from Fred all right.   Wish we'd a specimen of his handwriting.

MISS TRACEY.   We have.   (*She produces her notebook and from it the loose page.*)   I saw to that by asking him to write me a recipe for a cocktail.

EDNA (*looking at it*).   Nice work, Inspector Tracey. Looks a good cocktail, too.   Yes, that's Fred all right. (*She peers into the bag again and finally fishes out a tiny coloured envelope.*)   Calls itself a sample of our special face-powder.   I wonder.

(*She opens the envelope and pours a little of the powder into he palm of her hand. They look at it closely.*)

MISS TRACEY (*gravely*).   I think—it is what I was after.

EDNA.   Looks like it.

MISS TRACEY.   For herself, do you think?

EDNA.   No.   Just a sample—for customers.

MISS TRACEY.   That—seems to me—real, real, horrible wickedness.

EDNA.   Yes.   Not a nice girl at all.   I'm afraid our young assistant manager is in for a shock.

MISS TRACEY.   Yes—I noticed he was—well—impressed by her.   Don't be too hard on him, my dear.

EDNA.   Don't worry, I shan't.   (*She gets off the table, turns up* R., *then moves across back to* L.C.)   You see, I'm a—bit of a dam' fool myself—so I know—what it feels like.

MISS TRACEY (*quietly*).   I see.   (*She rises and comes a little* R., *then turns to* EDNA, *moving up* R. *With quick change of tone.*)   Funny how even clever wicked people give themselves away in little things, quite easily.   I asked her about Mrs. Morrison at Cannes, and she said—Oh—she thought Mrs. Morrison a darling and so sweet to her, when all the time I knew very well they hadn't got on at all.   It would have been much cleverer—and have given nothing away—if she'd said straight out that she and Mrs. Morrison couldn't hit it off.   I knew then she was a liar—at least.

EDNA.   And that was only the beginning of it.

(KEITH *enters* R., *looking rather miserable.*)

KEITH.   Crowther's all right.   Only he's not quite conscious.

EDNA.   He never was.

KEITH (*miserably*).   Sally says now that she knew that Helen Tennant and Fred met and talked late last night.   Who'd have thought a girl like that——

EDNA (*cutting in*).   Wait a minute.   (*Crossing in front of* MISS TRACEY *to* KEITH.)   You're making Sally's mistake.   Our society charmer wasn't condescending to have an affair with Fred, y'know. If that had been it, I'd have thought more about her——

MISS TRACEY (*surprised and shocked*). Miss Sandars, you wouldn't ! (*Coming* c. *above the table.*)

EDNA (*coolly*). Certainly I would. I'm the Modern Girl, y'know. You must have read about me. (*Turning to* KEITH *again.*) No, their relations were purely business ones. What Helen Tennant was doing, she was doing simply for money. People of her sort—who've been used to having plenty of money, and then suddenly find they haven't any—will do nearly anything for money, believe me.

KEITH (*earnestly, and abjectly*). Look here, I know I must have been a complete fool——

MISS TRACEY (*cutting in*). Mr. Henley, I've always wanted to hear a man say that. Now that I've heard it, I don't like it. Rather frightening. Don't say it again. (*She sits* c. *above the table.*)

KEITH. All right. But you two obviously know what's been happening, and I'm completely in the dark. I must be a bigger chump than I thought I was. Now, to begin with—where's Mrs. Jernigan ?

EDNA. Good Lord, I'd forgotten about that gag !

MISS TRACEY (*mock sternly*). Well, young woman, where *is* Mrs. Jernigan ?

EDNA (*coolly*). Oh, I'd settled that, last night, but I didn't see how you'd done it until this morning.

KEITH (*amazed*). How she'd done it ? Do you mean——

EDNA (*cutting in*). My dear Watson, my dear, dear Watson ! Now listen. An old lady is shown into a room. Then there are fireworks in that room. All the doors and windows are fastened on the inside. You break in and find that the old lady has disappeared, leaving behind a blood-stained handkerchief and one or two nice romantic clues. What's the explanation ? There can only be one possible explanation. Real old ladies can't disappear out of locked rooms. Therefore this wasn't a real old lady.

KEITH. But wait a minute——

MISS TRACEY (*ignoring him*). Did you suspect anything before the disappearance ?

EDNA. Yes. To start with, you seemed to me to be
behaving in a very complicated fashion. (*To* KEITH.)
I said so to you, but of course you were too busy dis-
approving of me to pay any real attention.

KEITH (*groaning*). Don't rub it in. (*He crosses up
stage to* L. *of the sideboard.*)

EDNA (*to* MISS TRACEY). I also noticed that both
elderly visitors had the same right heel.

MISS TRACEY (*chuckling*). And I said to myself, last
night, " That young woman's dangerous. She's got a
very sharp eye."

KEITH (*almost shouting*). Oh—just a minute, *please* !
D'you mean to say that *you* were Mrs. Jernigan ?
(*Coming down* L. *of the table.*)

MISS TRACEY. Of course I was.

EDNA. Instead of returning to her room, she went
back to the car, put on that comic hat and fur coat,
and came back with Clara as Mrs. Jernigan.

KEITH. But *why* ? (*Sitting* L. *of the table.*) What's
the sense in it ?

EDNA. Ah, that's what got me down.

MISS TRACEY. I'd two motives. The first—I'm
ashamed to say—though not *very* ashamed—was to
amuse myself and to see if a little scheme I'd worked
out could take anybody in. The second was quite a
serious motive, and I'll explain that later. (*Turning
to* EDNA, *chuckling.*) I don't think even you know how
I worked the disappearance.

EDNA. I didn't last night, but when I looked at
the room this morning, I did. You went in there as
Mrs. Jernigan, opened your bag and scattered the clues.
You locked both doors. Then you opened the window,
the one nearest to the door that led into your other
room, and tied some string to the catch of the window
and put the end of the string under the door into your
own room. Then you climbed out of the window, on
to the balcony, got into your own room, then pulled the
string under the door and that closed the window. Eh ?

MISS TRACEY (*chuckling*).   Right !   But how did I get rid of the string ?

KEITH.   Yes, there wasn't any string attached to the window.   And what about those three shots ?   You couldn't have fired them because you were down here talking to Crowther.

EDNA (*sitting on* R. *corner of the table, her back to the audience, and facing* MISS TRACEY).   That's where you had me guessing.

MISS TRACEY (*complacently*).   That was the really ingenious part of the scheme.   I'd worked it out just to amuse myself.   You see, the string I used to pull the window catch into place was also—a fuse.   I'd only to put a match to it, in my own room, and not only did it burn itself away, it also exploded three neat little bombs—they were like Chinese crackers—that were attached to the string.   It was a young nephew of mine, who dabbles in chemistry, who arranged all that for me.   So, once I'd lit the fuse, I could come away, talk to Crowther or anybody else, and have a perfect alibi.   Very ingenious, you must admit.

KEITH.   Very ingenious, Miss Tracey, but surely you don't go round England bewildering people with elaborate gadgets of this kind ?   You didn't come here just to play this trick on us, surely ?   I mean, it doesn't make sense.

EDNA.   I'll bet you don't like detective stories.

KEITH.   No, I don't—much.

EDNA.   I thought not.   I think she must have had a lot of fun, working that gag out.   Though of course that wasn't the only reason.

MISS TRACEY (*to* KEITH).   No.   You see, I deliberately followed Crowther here.   The reason he came at all was because I'd made a certain complaint to your head office.   But as soon as I knew they were sending Crowther round to all the company's hotels, I realized I'd have to do something myself, because I knew Crowther was a very stupid, hectoring sort of man.

EDNA.   So you gave him something to be getting on with ?   I saw that.

Miss Tracey. Not only that, my dear, but by creating this tremendous and ridiculous mystery, I made him set to work questioning everybody without putting the people I was really after *on their guard*. And by playing the fool myself, I was able to learn nearly all I wanted to know.

Edna. And you planted the Algiers address in Mrs. Jernigan's room just to worry them a bit.

Keith. Why, that was the address on the piece of paper Crowther said he found in my room.

Miss Tracey. Yes, I think the young man Fred put that there, this morning.

Keith. I knew somebody must have put it there. But does it mean anything ?

Miss Tracey (*gravely*). Yes, it was an address used by an agent of the drug traffic.

Keith (*rising—surprised and shocked*). Drug traffic ! But you don't mean——

Miss Tracey (*cutting in, seriously*). Yes, that is the real story. For the last year or so, supplies of a new drug—a synthetic alkaloid called " Serenaine," nearly as strong as cocaine, but cheaper—have been coming from the Near East. I know because a young cousin of mine nearly died from using it, this winter. It's just as foul and destructive as any of the old drugs.

Edna (*taking up the little envelope*). This is it.

Keith (*staring at the envelope and the bag*). Is that Helen Tennant's bag ?

Edna (*gently*). Yes, I'm afraid it is, Keith.

Miss Tracey. I knew that people had been getting this Serenaine at our hotel at Cannes. And I also knew that it wouldn't be long before these people began operating in England. For instance—here.

Keith (*slowly*). Fred and Helen Tennant were both at Cannes——

Miss Tracey. Yes, that's why I suspected them from the first. They were going to act as agents.

Edna. And I guessed this morning, from something that Clara and Sally had said.

KEITH (*to* EDNA). But how is it *you* knew about this drug business—and I didn't.

EDNA (*moving away* R. *and then back*). Oh—it wasn't from head office. It was from outside. You see, I have an uncle who's in the narcotic department of the C.I.D. and who sometimes works with the French police. He told me.

MISS TRACEY. By the way, while we're discussing your family, *was* your father the Chennelford who died in prison ?

EDNA. Good Lord, no ! I left that Chennelford letter in my room to keep Crowther amused. My name *is* Sandars, and my father's a country doctor. I'm the only member of the family who isn't respectable.

MISS TRACEY. You didn't rush away in Crowther's car just to buy the duplicate handbag, did you ?

EDNA. No, I rang up my uncle in town. And unless Helen Tennant and Fred are very lucky, I think they'll find themselves having a little talk to him to-morrow.

MISS TRACEY (*to* KEITH). I told you last night she was a very sharp young woman.

(*There is a noise off* R. *Sounds of* SALLY *and* CLARA *shouting* " Whoa ! " " Steady ! " *etc.* CROWTHER *staggers in, obviously still not quite himself after the blow and fall. His hair is wet and untidy, his collar loosened, etc., and he has a wild look.*)

CROWTHER (*wildly*). You're all—all of you—everybody—under arrest. (*He glares at them.*)

MISS TRACEY (*soothingly*). That's right, Mr. Crowther. We're all under arrest. Now have another nice lie down.

(CLARA *and* SALLY, *apparently enjoying themselves, rush on and take* CROWTHER *by the arms.*)

SALLY (*cajoling*). Now then, Mr. Crowther, you come and rest again, that's a good boy.

CLARA. And tell us some more about your Violet. (*She begins to lead him off.*)

SALLY (*turning, as she follows*). He once had a girl

called Violet. You ought to hear him on her! Talk about the Great Lover!

(*She goes out.* Keith, *amused, has followed them to the door.* Miss Tracey *comes down to him.* Edna *remains up* R.C.)

Miss Tracey. Poor Mr. Crowther! We'll have to give him some of the credit. He'll never know whether he's earned it or not. (*Turning to* Keith, *coolly.*) By the way, Mr. Henley, I shouldn't worry much about head office and your job here. You see, I had another reason still for coming here. Just to see what you were all like. This hotel and the one in Bournemouth are now run by a subsidiary company, and I happen to own a controlling interest in it. In fact, you might almost say this is my hotel.

Keith. Good Lord—and I've been——

Miss Tracey. That's all right.

(*The telephone rings, rather startlingly.*)

Edna. Hello, the relief force has got through.

Miss Tracey. Yes, and I'm going to answer it.

(*She hurries out* L.)

Keith (*ruefully*). I seem to have been the king chump of the world. You must think me an awful fool.

Edna (*cheerfully, coming to* R. *end of the table*). I do, but then I'm a bit of a fool myself.

Keith (*wonderingly*). You seem to me the most extraordinary girl I've ever met.

Edna. Now you keep on talking like that, and I'll be coming round every five minutes for more. And—please notice—my nose isn't bad. (*Showing her profile.*) Is it?

Keith. No, it's a very amusing nose.

Edna (*bringing her face closer still*). Take a good look at it.

(Miss Tracey *bursts in rather dramatically.*)

Miss Tracey. There, there, life goes on.

EDNA. What was it ?
MISS TRACEY. Wrong number !

(*All three laugh.*)

QUICK CURTAIN.

FURNITURE PLOT

1 dining-table.
5 dining-chairs.
3 small armchairs.
2 small tables.
1 sideboard.
1 console radio set.

PROPERTY PLOT

On Stage

ACT I

Staff letter-rack with 3 or 4 letters.
Staff notice-board with 2 or 3 notices.
Staff FIRE regulations notice.
" Radio Times."
Stenographer's notebook and pencil for HELEN.
Magazines.
Table laid with remains of supper for five.
Bottles, etc., on sideboard.

ACT II

Stenographer's notebook and pencil for EDNA.

ACT III

Dummy revolver on table.

Off Stage

ACT I

Revolver with blanks.
Large tray for CLARA.
Bottle of rum for FRED.
Small pad and pencil for FRED.
Cup of tea on small tray for CLARA.
Small suitcase for CROWTHER.
Suitcase for MISS TRACEY.
Handbag for HELEN.
Suitcase for MRS. JERNIGAN.
Large sandwich for CLARA.
Newspaper and pocket-flask for CROWTHER.
Plate of sandwiches, small jug of water and tumbler on tray
    for CLARA.

ACT II

Envelope containing two torn pieces of letter for CROWTHER.
Cup of coffee for EDNA.
2 doorkeys for EDNA.

ACT III

Saucer of flour for CLARA.
Handbag—duplicate of HELEN's in Act I—containing letters and
    envelope of white powder—for EDNA.
Small loaded revolver for MISS TRACEY.